Preaching *and* Praying
as though God Matters

"In a time when the cold winds of skepticism and disenchantment blow hard, both outside the church and in it as well, Ron Byars has written a bold, encouraging, and hopeful book. He finds deeps wells of wisdom in the church's liturgy, and he allows that wisdom to summon the kind of preaching that is desperately needed in today's world—preaching that courageously announces the hope God alone can bring. Bravo!"
— THOMAS G. LONG,
Candler School of Theology, emeritus

"The Reformers emphasized the preaching of the word to save the abuse of the sacrament. In this book, Ron Byars asks whether in our time, when words are cheap and so much preaching dissolves in therapeutic or moralistic reflections, the sacrament might not serve the church's proclamation. With the voice of a theologian and the heart of a preacher, Byars explores the church's eucharistic prayers to unfold the riches of the gospel."
— EDWIN CHR. VAN DRIEL,
Pittsburgh Theological Seminary

"By grounding preaching in Scripture and eucharistic theology, Byars achieves an integration among the chief elements of worship and orients the whole to 'things at the center.' Extended examples from actual sermons demonstrate how preaching can be theologically probing and also compelling to contemporary audiences."
— ELLEN F. DAVIS,
Duke Divinity School

"With wisdom and conviction, Byars addresses subjects too often divided—sermon and sacraments—as interdependent and mutually illuminating elements of the church's worship. He draws on a host of biblical, liturgical, historical, and theological sources to present a compelling vision for preaching and prayer in our contemporary context. To this great cloud of witnesses, Byars adds his own voice, informed by a lifetime of experience as a preacher, presider, pastor, professor, and person of prayer."
— DAVID GAMBRELL,
associate for worship, Office of Theology and Worship, Presbyterian Church (U.S.A.)

"A compelling interdependence of word and sacrament is an aspirational goal for most Protestant worship. We need to hear voices from across the spectrum of Protestant traditions exploring what it could mean to practice this interdependence. Ron Byars takes up this challenge, exploring a dynamic variety of biblical, theological, and historical dimensions of liturgical renewal, challenging us to entrust our ministries to the enduring work of the Holy Spirit through the means of grace."

—JOHN WITVLIET,
Calvin Institute of Christian Worship

"Ronald Byars has gifted us with an articulate and comprehensive presentation of the meaning of Christian eschatological faith, as not about me getting to heaven, but rather about God's promise of cosmic redemption, and as encountered in the word, proclaimed and preached, and the sacramental meal shared by the assembly."

—GAIL RAMSHAW,
author of *Pray, Praise, and Give Thanks*

"Ron Byars has given us another gem with his dazzling combination of pastoral insight, cultural criticism, historical knowledge, and theological acumen. He shows how careful attention to the liturgy, particularly eucharistic prayers, can shape the lives of preachers and congregations. Years of ministry undergird these reflections. Byars' mature faith and love for his subject remain fresh. Pastors will enjoy his personal reflections on the pastoral life. This is a feast sustains the mind and heart."

—ROY HOWARD,
Academy of Artful Leadership

Preaching *and* Praying *as Though* God Matters

In the Post-establishment Church

Ronald P. Byars

Foreword by Don E. Saliers

CASCADE *Books* • Eugene, Oregon

PREACHING AND PRAYING AS THOUGH GOD MATTERS
In the Post-establishment Church

Copyright © 2022 Ronald P. Byars. All rights reserved. Except for brief quotations in critical publications or reviews, no part of this book may be reproduced in any manner without prior written permission from the publisher. Write: Permissions, Wipf and Stock Publishers, 199 W. 8th Ave., Suite 3, Eugene, OR 97401.

Cascade Books
An Imprint of Wipf and Stock Publishers
199 W. 8th Ave., Suite 3
Eugene, OR 97401

www.wipfandstock.com

PAPERBACK ISBN: 978-1-6667-4709-6
HARDCOVER ISBN: 978-1-6667-4710-2
EBOOK ISBN: 978-1-6667-4711-9

Cataloguing-in-Publication data:

Names: Byars, Ronald P., author. | Saliers, Don E., 1937–, foreword.

Title: Preaching and praying as though God matters : in the post-establishment church / Ronald P. Byars.

Description: Eugene, OR: Cascade Books, 2022. | Includes bibliographical references and index.

Identifiers: ISBN 978-1-6667-4709-6 (paperback). | ISBN 978-1-6667-4710-2 (hardcover). | ISBN 978-1-6667-4711-9 (ebook).

Subjects: LCSH: Preaching. | Prayer. | Christianity—21st century. | Spiritual life—Christianity. | Discipleship.

Classification: BX4805.3 B933 2022 (print). | BX4805.3 (epub).

Scripture quotations are from New Revised Standard Version Bible, copyright © 1989 National Council of the Churches of Christ in the United States of America. Used by permission. All rights reserved worldwide.

Figure 1: Anastasis, Harrowing of Hell and Resurrection (eleventh-century fresco). Self-photographed by GunnarBach, February 2004. https://commons.wikimedia.org/wiki/File:Chora_Anastasis1.jpg

This book is dedicated to Susan, my life's companion,
and to Steve and Lisa, Grace and Ben
Matt and Melissa, Jonas and Audrey

As we communicate in the Sacrament, we participate in the new time of [the] Kingdom. That is why the New Testament thinks of the sacraments as falling within the overlap between the two ages, this present age that passes away and the age that is to come but which in Christ has already telescoped into the present and catches us up into it in the Communion of the Spirit.

—THOMAS F. TORRANCE, *SPACE, TIME AND RESURRECTION*

Contents

Foreword by Don E. Saliers | viii

Introduction | 1

1. The Challenge of Preaching in a Post-Establishment Church | 16
2. Preaching What Is Prayed: The Renewal of All Things | 30
3. The Reformation: Preaching to Get Ready for Heaven | 45
4. Preaching the Cosmic Scope of God's Redemption | 60
5. Preaching and Its Trinitarian Foundation | 71
6. Christological Preaching | 90
7. Preaching the Holy Spirit and the Messianic Banquet | 110
8. Preaching When Naiveté Has Fled | 123

Afterword | 134

Bibliography | 141

Foreword

FEW RECENT BOOKS ON preaching and worship have opened the intimate connection between word and sacrament as powerfully and as accessibly as this one. Ron Byars has invited us to a feast at once biblical, historical, theological, and pastoral. Honestly assessing the current cultural situation of mainline Christian churches in America, these pages address essential questions for all who preach and lead worship. Why and how can we pray in a skeptical time? How can our all-too-human words convey faith? Why are preaching and the sacrament of the Lord's table intimately related? What can we learn from the strengths and limitations of the Protestant and Roman Catholic "reformations"? Is it possible to regain the word of God, proclaimed and heard, by understanding and practicing the gospel pattern found in the central prayer of the Eucharist?

In our generation, Christians must discern for our time and circumstances what theological "misunderstandings" we carry. Carefully, layer by layer, Byars illuminates how we may approach this task. Even more importantly, he draws us to how we may participate in the depth of God's self-giving in word and sacrament. Drawing upon a deft, accessible analysis of the ecumenical recovery of the shape and content of Eucharistic prayers, he offers a challenging argument: preaching must take its cues and energy from those prayers and actions. He invites us how to preach (and to "hear") matters at the heart of Christian faith by learning to pray more deeply at the Lord's Table.

Along the way we learn central things about Reformation doctrine and doxology, the work of the Spirit, the necessity of Trinitarian preaching, and the cosmic scope of redemption. Into each distinctive chapter are enfolded examples from the author's own sermons. The "preacher's reflections" alone are worth the whole book—full of insightful exegesis, and always sharply

Foreword

to the point. The reader is compelled to dive deeply into the stories and images we pray and preach. I found myself affirming afresh that worship is not a classroom, nor a concert hall, nor is the Bible a simple textbook. Rather, Christian worship is presence and prophetic engagement with the living God of Scripture in this present world of suffering and glory. In these pages we find a much-needed sacramental theology of the word of God for a "post-establishment" church.

While this book is addressed to those who preach and lead worship, it is clearly a book for anyone seeking insight about Christian faith and worship today. I say, "Take up and read!"

Don E. Saliers

Cannon Prof. of Theology and Worship, Emeritus,
and Theologian-in-Residence, Emory University

Introduction

What the Pandemic Taught Us

THE LAST SERVICE IN our church before the COVID-19 pandemic hit was on March 8, 2020. It would be more than a year until we were invited to return to the sanctuary in person, under certain conditions: make a reservation (limited numbers), wear a mask, social distancing, no singing by the congregation, no offering plate passed, no Eucharist. We made the effort, even though it made for an earlier morning than we had grown used to; we needed to dress more carefully to leave the house, and, though vaccinated, we were taking a measured risk that we were not used to taking. My spouse and I entered by a door from the education building, meaning that we came in from the front of the sanctuary, facing the pews. All at once, we saw people we had not seen in more than a year. We saw them from the nose up, masked. The sight struck me emotionally in a way that I had not experienced before when coming to church using that same entry.

We were not allowed to sing for the first three Sundays, while a small group from the choir sang the hymns for us, masked. As they began to sing, I was grateful for my own mask, because not only were my eyes filled with tears, but I was shaking the pew with smothered sobs. When the worshiping assembly is part of a normal weekly routine, it is natural to take it for granted. We may not even know that week by week, we are accumulating a set of experiences that are being laid down in layers in our unconscious minds. We are absorbing by a kind of osmosis a series of impressions from our surroundings, scarcely noted in the moment, including color, furnishings, symbols, sounds, actions, and, most important, the presence of other people, all accompanied by emotions most often not cognitively registered. Even if one faithfully watches a service online, many of those experiences are missing entirely, or in the case of those that are adaptable to a computer screen, they affect one differently by the fact that they are miniaturized and no longer part of a whole liturgical ecology. Each experience, when removed or taken out of context, alters the perception of the whole in some way.

The parts of the liturgy that remain in an online service tend to be highlighted by those that are directed to our thinking and reasoning selves. Or, if not quite that, they are the parts that can be most easily expressed in words. Words matter, of course. They are not insignificant, and need to be chosen carefully. But words are most effective when embedded in a series of actions in a holistic environment, drawing upon layers of our bodily and spiritual experience that influence us enormously without our being tuned into them consciously.

For the Mainline Churches, "Established" Status Is Over

Under scrutiny, it seems evident that even in our usual worship spaces and following familiar patterns, something has been lost, and the losses precede the pandemic. One of those losses is the confidence that accompanied the sense that "mainline" churches would always enjoy a kind of unofficial "establishment" status in the mostly Protestant (USA). Clearly, the culture has withdrawn any such privilege. But there is an even more existential loss. It is hard to put a finger on it, but that loss seems to be whatever it is that we were once able to bring to our worshiping assemblies—maybe a sense of trust. In other words, the dominant culture has changed, slowly enough that it has been hard to notice, but none of us has been left untouched. What once came naturally may now seem forced, or even false.

In several other writings I have tried to unfold what I think has happened.[1] We are not the same culture, not the same people that we were in the sixteenth century, or the nineteenth, or even in the mid-twentieth. For many reasons, faith of any kind is more often met with skepticism in contemporary society than it used to be. For one thing, our society is suspicious of institutions generally, and we are taught to be on the lookout for signs that we are being deceived. Any claim upon us is likely to be evaluated in that light. Does this person or this authority claim that they believe something to be true? Particularly in an era suspicious of faith, they need

1. Byars, *Believer on Sunday*; Byars, *Sacraments*; Byars, *Finding Our Balance*.

Introduction

to prove it. And, in this culture the default setting for proving anything is either to produce objective evidence or a reasoned argument sufficient to overcome objections.

Actually, it is hard enough to do that consistently in any area of thought, including the sciences, but it is especially difficult in reference to holy things. In terms of Christian faith, and other faiths as well, God is not a phenomenon within the universe, but its creator, and therefore beyond either evidential proof or satisfactory explanation in language that sprang into being to deal with temporal matters. If we are to "know" God at all, it will almost certainly involve engaging those layered parts of ourselves that lie below the surface, feeding the intellect and being fed by it, yes, but overflowing the capacities of the intellect alone. Objectivity serves its purposes; but there is also a place for that part of us that is intuitive, for insights that reach us otherwise than by a reasonable syllogism.

> Every one of us experiences more input from our environment than we are capable of recognizing and paying attention to. Lots of incoming data cannot be processed by the conscious, evaluating mind at the moment of input. There is simply too much of it. To "receive" it all at once would overload our circuits. Our conscious minds just have to filter lots of it out, paying attention only to those small bits we can absorb at the moment. But that does not mean that all the data we filter out does not affect us at some level. We "know" more than we are processing consciously, and more than we can put into words.[2]

Working Out Our Relationship with the Dominant Culture

The culture in which we are all immersed has formed our expectations, even in church. We do not entirely trust the faith we have, because we are pressed to put every truth claim to the test. In these circumstances, doubt comes at least as easily as faith, and because it really matters, we are not at ease with ambiguity. The liturgy of the church is one in which Christ is the liturgist, guiding us as we express faith both personal and shared by the communion of saints that includes generations present and past. It is meant both to provide a vehicle by which to offer praise, thanksgiving, and intercession, but also an immersion experience in which we as a specific

---

2. Byars, *Believer on Sunday*, 33.

faith community are being formed, shaped, supported, and mentored in the faith of the church. This faith is already ours, and yet it continues to be a work in progress, requiring a lifetime to reach maturity. A liturgy both expressive and formative requires the use of two side-by-side and layered languages: the language of the head, and the language of the heart. These are not opposed to one another, but each touches us somewhat differently, and together they engage us holistically. The apostle Paul understood the need for both, and while he reasoned with those who learned the faith from him, he also prayed that the Ephesian believers would have "the eyes of your heart[s] enlightened" (Eph 1:18).

Those who plan and lead worship as well as those who preach live in the same world as the congregation does, and are not immune from its pressures. Even the church's appointed leaders may rightfully feel defensive in today's culture, and defensiveness can lead to timidity in place of confidence. Preachers may feel just a little less pressure when ways can be found to circumvent some of the more challenging parts of the church's faith. Once I was pastor of a relatively new congregation. The members were young, as I was, and many of them were educators or staff members at a university nearby. One Easter Sunday, a visitor from out of town, older than I, introduced himself to me at the door after the service. He had an authoritative demeanor, and kindly tried to help me out, explaining that it made no sense for me to be preaching about the resurrection to this young, well-educated congregation. I guess he assumed that he and I shared a learned skepticism, but that I was too timid to come right out and say so. Better, maybe, to find something Easter-ish to say that might be passable to presumed skeptics?

Of course, it is not safe for one's soul (not to mention integrity) to offer an alternative gospel that is less likely to offend settled opinions in a congregation. In a recent conference at a retreat center, one person present had a question for the presenter of the day. He reported that some people in the congregation of which he was a part had objected to the Apostles' and Nicene creeds on the grounds that they didn't entirely agree with either of them. "Why shouldn't we stop saying the creed?" he asked. The presenter, a church musician, responded that it is mistaken to imagine that the only possible position was either to believe or to doubt. The fact is, we all both believe and doubt at the same time. True. And one might add that, should we abandon everything about which one or many may have doubts, settled or occasional, we would have nothing to say at all.

INTRODUCTION

While our Easter visitor may or may not have assessed either me or the congregation accurately, any pastor nevertheless understands that the resurrection is one of the hard parts, as are incarnation, healings of the sick, giving sight to the blind, raising people from the dead, and the cross itself, not to mention the resurrection of the Lord. Understanding the difficulty, we look for ways to deal with those challenging texts that we will certainly run across if we are using the lectionary. Of course, there are always ways of taming the hard texts—for example, de-theologizing them—turning a challenging text into a moral lesson or social commentary. Minimizing the hard parts may reassure skeptics in the congregation that the church is reasonable enough, after all, suitably updated, really a kind of school and support group for people interested in ethical and social questions. All good, if the object is to save the institution even if it means throwing under the bus its Lord and its *raison d'être*.

An Unexpected Question: "Do You Believe in God?"

The writer and preacher, Fleming Rutledge, reports a conversation she had during a lunch with someone whose own writing interested her. At some point, he asked her, "Do you believe in God?" An unexpected question, addressed to a member of the clergy. Yet Rutledge describes her own experience:

> I have heard sermons from Maine to Florida, from Boston to Honolulu, from New Orleans to Minneapolis. No exaggeration. Therefore, I speak with a certain amount of authority when I say that there are a lot of clergy out there who give every impression of not believing in God. By that I don't mean that the word *God* is not mentioned. What I mean is that God plays only a subsidiary or vague role in the messages. . . . The subject in so much of our preaching is ourselves—our faith, our 'spirituality', our works, our journeys, our responsibilities, our needs, our ministries.[3]

To the extent that Rutledge is right, "belief" in God is not always evident in preaching, but neither is it always evident in a liturgy created just for the day either. Mainline Protestants, hardly noticed by the greater part of society any longer, have managed to define themselves to each other as the anything-but-fundamentalist churches, the not-wed-to-the-right-wing folks. As the several mainline denominations meld into a shared kind of

---

3. Rutledge, *And God Spoke*, 259, 260.

anything-but category, it feels as though we are experiencing what might be called a thinning out of the "hard parts." Mainline churches seem to be leaning toward theological and sacramental minimalism, too easily conforming to the enlightenment-shaped culture that thinks of the "truth" as available only by means of objective evidence that must be processed intellectually, and justified by the intellect alone.

Impressionistic evidence is that today mainline preaching is being affected by the temptation to minimize, and so is worship. My proposal in this book is that we look once again to liturgical theology to take us by the hand and lead us to a recovery of solid theological substance. Most importantly, leading us to the God in whom we have claimed to rest our trust. That theologically substantial, God-centered witness is embedded in the liturgical texts that are most likely to be found in the several most recent denominational service books. They are particularly evident in the newer eucharistic prayers (Great Thanksgivings) that have appeared in the books of various denominations since the Second Vatican Council in the 1960s. The Great Thanksgivings at the altar/table are often reliable guides to biblical basics, and particularly to the eschatological images that are being revisited and welcomed again by theologians both Protestant and Catholic.

Liturgical theology, like other kinds, is both conservative and liberalizing. "Conservative" in the sense that it can remind us of important things that we may have grown used to ignoring, to the point that they have become lost for all practical purposes. But they are also liberalizing in the sense that liturgical theology is an instrument that can be called upon to support necessary reform. It can wake us up, draw our attention when something has become obscured, misunderstood, blown out of proportion or minimized. To begin to recover affirmations basic to the Christian faith in our preaching and in our worship, we would do well to look carefully at that treasure easily accessible in newer denominational service books. They conserve by bringing to view things that had fallen out of sight; and they frame those forgotten things for new generations to notice.

The Reformers brought preaching in from the margins to serve a sacramental purpose every Lord's Day. It may be that, at the time of the Reformation, the recovery of preaching in every Sunday service had the effect of serving, along with other purposes, as a kind of rescue-mission for the sacraments. Preaching modeled what "sacramental" means vividly enough to save the sacraments from superstition or obscurantism. One wonders

Introduction

whether something like that might be possible again now, but this time it might be the Eucharist that comes to the rescue of preaching.

Eucharistic Prayer Shows a Way

In this book, I am particularly interested in eucharistic prayer and what a careful examination of it might mean for those who take the risk of preaching in the twenty-first century. The preacher may benefit by respect for the Trinitarian substance of eucharistic prayer, as well as its consistent thanksgiving for the mighty acts of God as represented in biblical narratives. Preaching may become less narrow, less cautious, and offer a grander view when eucharistic prayer models the renewed accent on a cosmic and universal redemption that is exemplified in the eschatological expectation of the reign of Christ, the kingdom of God, the *parousia* (return of Christ) leading to the *basileia*, a new heaven and earth. These reflections can lead us to more confident preaching of the "central things," marked by both a generous orthodoxy and an expansive and welcoming "big picture."

Included in various moves throughout the book will be "a preacher's reflections," mostly from my own lightly edited sermons and provided here as food for thought for those preaching on specific biblical narratives named or alluded to in the Great Thanksgivings. They may also be useful for teaching congregations about the magnificent prayer that they will be expected to affirm with their "Amen." Teaching the liturgy matters. Every reformation starts with rediscovering the power of sources, and the sources begin with the Bible itself, the ecumenical creeds (Apostles' and Nicene), and two millennia of ecclesiastical experience in liturgical praise and thanksgiving. In the twenty-first century, liturgical theology may be the right countercultural tool to help us to engage with those basic sources for reform and renewal once again. That source-based theology is heartily represented in the service books already on our shelves. There is delight to be found in them and in the ways they serve to alert us to look for the sacramental dimensions of both preaching and worship, just as there is delight in the uplifted heart.

> Lift up your hearts!
> *We lift them to the Lord!*

A Note on Engaging with Scripture

At some point, everyone who expects to preach needs to come to terms with the challenge of the Bible. Those who arrive at seminary without having had an academic introduction to the study of Scripture often experience a sense of shock in their first course on Old or New Testament. Presuming that their pre-seminary church experience was in one of the mainline denominations, they are not likely to have been taught any particular theory about the nature of the Bible. They were not taught that every word came directly from God, or that a choice needs to be made between believing in science or believing in the literal factuality of the creation stories in Genesis. And yet, it still comes as a surprise to learn the complexities of the Bible's origins and all the details of the various schools of thought about how to take it apart to understand it: form criticism, redaction criticism, historical criticism, and whatever other criticisms there may be! "New Testament scholar Leander Keck cites a comment made by a student who had been a lay preacher before beginning formal theological study: 'I could preach a whole lot better before I took your [New Testament Interpretation] course.'"[4]

A student either finds a way to work through this exposure to new information without losing faith, or does not, with or without the help of the faculty member teaching the course. My experience is limited, but my impression is that many faculty find ways to help the novice to integrate new information in ways that are supportive to faith. Others, no doubt including New Testament professor Luke Timothy Johnson, judge otherwise, perhaps influenced by the preaching of some of those who demonstrate unfortunate effects after their exposure to biblical scholarship. Johnson's view is that

> Rationalistic skepticism characterizes the classic historical-critical approach to the Old and New Testaments: academic engagement with miracle stories tends to be dismissive when it appears at all. . . . Such a reductionist approach, in turn, is inculcated (sometimes flagrantly, sometimes subtly) in the study of the Bible in seminaries and schools of theology."[5]

Johnson is no fundamentalist. Presumably he is registering observations of what he has seen and heard in classrooms, as well as what he has heard from mainline pulpits. He is highlighting the fact that ways of

---

4. Davis, *Wondrous Depth*, 63.
5. Johnson, *Miracles*, 19.

Introduction

interpreting Scripture under the pervasive authority of Enlightenment standards has led to academic norms shaped by the scientific model of taking a thing apart in order to understand it. A case can be made that to understand something, taking it apart serves a purpose, particularly if it is a machine, but the machine model of the universe that served Newtonian physics well enough does not stand up so well in an era of quantum physics. When one takes anything apart, including a text, one may learn something about the separate parts and how they are related to each other. But one may lose a sense of the whole. The power of a text is best perceived and experienced holistically as one encounters the finished (canonical) text itself.

Is There a Word from the Lord?

Faculty will find it necessary to introduce students to the established methods of the professional guild. But preparing students for the personal engagement of the text necessary for preaching requires a step beyond employment of historical and literary analysis. How does one hear a particular text as, in some sense, a word from the Lord?

Johnson, for example, writes about "miracles" that they should be understood "less as unassailable facts to which all must consent and more as deeply ambiguous signals that require a transformed imagination to be perceived."[6] In any case, he and others like him affirm that God is at work in the world, and revealed in Scripture. "The miraculous is not, as modernity would have it, an exception to the well-established laws of nature, but is rather the magic of God's power and presence, whose laws or logic humans must struggle to decipher."[7]

Apart from what may or may not happen in the classroom, it remains true that the prevailing skepticism in matters of faith poses a challenge for everyone, but certainly for the preacher, who is trying to make sense of a Bible that is focused on a God who is somehow engaged with the world and with us. Narratives that are basic to Christian faith make claims that simply do not square with the norms that the dominant culture finds acceptable. That requires us, at the very least, to wrestle with how to understand the mysterious languages of Scripture. Did Jesus *really* walk on water? Still the storm? Feed the multitudes? Give sight to the blind? Raise the dead? If not *really*, then metaphorically, symbolically? If *really*, do we need to support

---

6. Johnson, *Miracles*, 94.
7. Johnson, *Miracles*, 62.

that view by embracing a theory of historicity rooted in a claim of textual infallibility? Or is there another way to look at these questions?

One of the persistent questions about the New Testament is what to make of the stories that describe Jesus and his ministry when he does things that seem beyond ordinary possibility. Of course, the New Testament writers were remembering the story of Jesus' life and ministry retrospectively, looking backward through the lens of the resurrection. The cross may have caused grief and dismay, but the resurrection refocused the view of his story from beginning to triumphant climax. Reflecting on it from a resurrection point of view no doubt motivated early interpreters to reflect on the details of his pre-resurrection life through opened eyes.

It helps to understand the significant role the Old Testament plays in interpreting Jesus in the New Testament. The writers of the New Testament bear a testimony about Jesus that, by the very nature of a testimony, is and has to be an interpretation of who he was and what he was about. Because he was a Jew, it was natural for those trying to tell his story to do it contextually, making use of Old Testament stories, allusions, and images in the art of interpreting who Jesus was and is. For example, Matthew and Luke both engaged in speculation about his conception and birth, as though certainly there must have been clues to his identity and mission vouchsafed to some witness or witnesses from the very beginning. How could such a momentous event possibly have gone completely unnoticed, particularly by Mary and Joseph? Matthew interprets Jesus as another Moses, his life at stake at the hands of a ruthless ruler and baby-killer, Herod this time in place of Moses' Pharaoh. The holy family escapes the potential slaughter by seeking shelter in Egypt until the coast seems to be clear. The Gospel reinforces those inter-testamental connections with part of a quote from Hos 11:1. Matthew cites it, in reference to Jesus, as "Out of Egypt I have called my son" (2:15). The whole sentence from Hosea reads, "When Israel was a child, I loved him, and out of Egypt I called my son." So, the Gospel suggests that Jesus is equivalent to a new Moses, a new Israel, and entitled to the descriptor, "son," an extension of "son" language expanded from Israel to include Jesus.

The story of Jesus walking on water, found in Matt 14:24, Mark 6:45–52, and John 6:1–13 is likely a reiteration of the story of Israel fleeing from Egypt, crossing the sea to safety. "Your way was through the sea, your path, through the mighty waters; yet your footprints were unseen (Ps 77:19). Similarly, "Thus says the LORD [Hebrew *YHWH*], who makes a way in the sea, a path in the mighty waters" (Isa 43:16). In the New Testament walking on water scenes, the Gospel writers evoke memories of Old Testament texts to identify Jesus as one who embodies and recapitulates the experience of Israel and, at the same time identifying him with "the Lord, who makes a way in the sea."

All three Synoptic Gospels tell the story of Jesus stilling the storm (Matt 8:23–27; Mark 4:35–41; Luke 8:22–25). The story evokes Ps 89, in which the psalmist addresses God, saying, "You rule the raging of the sea; when its waves rise, you still them" (89:7), and Ps 107, "Then they cried to the Lord in their trouble, and he brought them out from their distress; he made the storm be still, and the waves of the sea were hushed" (107:28–29). The Gospel writers are summoning Old Testament images to tell us who Jesus is. He is "ruler of all nature," as the hymn "Fairest Lord Jesus" sums it up so lyrically.

In the various stories of the feeding of the multitudes (for example, Matt 14:13–21; Mark 6:30–44; Luke 9:10–17; John 6:1–13), the Gospel writers are linking Jesus with the two prophets, Elijah and Elisha, each of whom similarly fed a large number of people with scant supplies (1 Kgs 17:7–16; 2 Kgs 4:42–44).

A particularly striking feature of some of the Gospels is when Jesus is reported to have used the telling phrase "I am" to refer to himself. The phrase is noteworthy because of Moses' experience in the encounter with the bush that was burning, but not consumed (Exod 3). A voice spoke to Moses out of the burning bush, calling him to a position of leadership. Moses wanted to know what he should say should the people ask from whom this call to leadership had come. The voice in the bush answered, "I am who I am" . . . "Thus you shall say to the Israelites, I am has sent me to you" (3:14). When Jesus is in the Garden of Gethsemane, soldiers and police came searching for him. Jesus asked them for whom they were looking, and they answered, "Jesus of Nazareth." Jesus replied, "I am he." (In the Greek, "I am.") "When Jesus said to them, 'I am he,' they stepped back and fell to the ground" (John 18:6). John imagines those coming to arrest Jesus as falling into a state of shock when confronted with his "Ego eimi." "I am" kindled an alarm in these dutiful officers, for whom the story of Moses' ancient encounter was foundational. The drama as John describes it is obviously intended to highlight for the reader Jesus' identity with the One revealed to Moses. Similar uses of "I am" can be found a number of times in the Gospel of John and elsewhere.

The Old Testament offers several examples of prophets complaining that the people are without a shepherd. "Ah, you shepherds of Israel, who have been feeding yourselves!" (Ezek 34:2). Ezekiel accuses those who are meant to play a caretaking role of having exploited what was meant to be a servant position.

> You have not strengthened the weak,
> you have not healed the sick,
> you have not bound up the injured,
> you have not brought back the strayed,
> you have not sought the lost,
> but with force and harshness you have ruled them (34:4).

In the same chapter, an exasperated Ezekiel writes, "For thus says the Lord God: I myself will search out my sheep, and will seek them out . . . I myself will be the shepherd of my sheep (34:11 and 15). Mark's Gospel, telling the story of the feeding of a multitude, describes Jesus' compassion for the crowd, "because they were like sheep without a shepherd" (6:34). Jesus organizes the crowd, directing them "to sit down in groups on the green grass" (6:39). This is certainly reminiscent of Psalm 23, "The Lord (Hebrew: *YHWH*) is my shepherd, I shall not want. He makes me lie down in green pastures" (23:1–2a). And John reports Jesus as saying, "I am the good shepherd. The good shepherd lays down his life for the sheep" (John 10:11), both reiterating the "I am" and identifying Jesus with the declaration recorded by Ezekiel and linked directly to God's own promise, "*I myself* will be the shepherd of my sheep."

Jesus Interpreted

So, Jesus reenacts the gift of manna to feed the hungry in the wilderness. He is characterized as the new Moses, new Israel, new Elijah and Elisha, reliable shepherd strengthening the weak, healing the sick, binding up the injured, bringing back the strayed, seeking the lost, the one rightly identified as "I am."

These are only a few of many possible examples of how the New Testament witnesses interpreted Jesus using images and parallels from the Old Testament. Richard Bauckham has argued against the conventionalities of New Testament scholarship that have worked from the premise that much of what we find there was created by and for the later church rather than derived directly from the lifetime of Jesus. Bauckham's studies draw

Introduction

attention to the fact that eyewitnesses play an important part in a largely oral culture, as they did in Jesus' time and do even now in traditional Palestinian society. Such societies follow unwritten rules about the transmission of stories. The rules vary depending on the nature of what is intended to be handed on, but "The disciples of rabbis were expected to memorize their master's teaching, and importance was attached to preserving the exact words."[8] "In short, while the Gospels undoubtedly give us Jesus *interpreted* (fact and fiction necessarily co-inhere in all understanding of the past . . .), the interpretation is very largely of the eyewitnesses themselves and of the Gospel writers."[9] Bauckham argues that it is illusory to believe that "it was possible to get back to an uninterpreted Jesus behind all the interpretations to which he was subjected in the creative process of the transmission of the traditions."[10] In other words, the effort to get behind the Gospel texts themselves to discover an uninterpreted Jesus is a fool's errand. Garrett Green's opinion is that "If we want to know the facts to which the story refers, we can only respond that they 'are facts that we cannot have apart from the story.'"[11]

My own view is indebted to the late Hans Frei and to some who have learned from him. He thought "that many of the episodes in the Gospels function as illustrative anecdotes: They show us the sort of person Jesus was, whether or not this particular incident took place."[12] Frei adds that "we must try for a reading in which the text itself is the meaning, the narrative form indispensable to the narrative's meaning."[13] For example, we cannot really know what experience lies behind the story of Jesus walking on water. But the narrative is clear enough that we can know the various dimensions of what the story *means*—i.e., what it intends to say. The Gospel narratives adequately serve their intended purpose, and it is those narratives with which we need to deal.

However, in Frei's view, Jesus' resurrection "must, in the eyes of those who believe, be a factual occurrence of a wholly unique kind."[14] We don't have to make an historical judgment about what happened in the feeding of

---

8. Bauckham, *Jesus and the Eyewitnesses*, 249.
9. Bauckham, *Jesus and the Eyewitnesses*, 615.
10. Bauckham, *Jesus and the Eyewitnesses*, 611.
11. Green, *Imagining Theology*, 86.
12. Frei, *Theology and Narrative*, 13.
13. Frei, *Theology and Narrative*, 41.
14. Frei, *Theology and Narrative*, 47.

the multitudes, or about the details surrounding Jesus' birth, but the resurrection does not fall into the same category as those. Even the stories about which we do not have to make up our minds are nevertheless coherent with the Jesus known in cross and resurrection.

Some scholars, including Luke Timothy Johnson, cited earlier, use the term "myth" to describe stories that seem to stretch the possibility of being literally "true" in an objective historical manner, but nevertheless still communicate a truth. But Hans Frei rejects the use of "myth" to describe the New Testament narratives about Jesus, because "myth" is inherently generic. It implies a "truth" that could be recognized apart from a particular narrative, either in an alternative story or as a "truth" that might be expressed in general, discursive language. But, for Frei, the Gospel narratives do not embody generic "truths," but "together they conspire to describe and affirm the identity of a particular, concrete individual."[15] Jesus is not simply a religious symbol. "The genre of the gospel narrative is therefore precisely the opposite of that of myth."[16]

For the preacher, "[T]he subject matter of the Bible is [in] the text, rather than . . . [in] the peripheries that were behind the text, which was what historical criticism did."[17] Green argues that twentieth-century theologian "[Karl] Barth's ambition—and Frei's—is 'to be a *direct* reader of the text, and not of some hypothetical subject matter behind the text.' One reads this way 'not as an uncritically naïve reader but as a critically naïve reader.'"[18]

Ellen Davis has expressed the opinion that "the text appears more wondrous when viewed through the lens of the Christian tradition of theology and liturgy. . . . With eyes and mind enriched by gifts of insight received from our predecessors, we begin to see, not a single fixed meaning, but the abundance of potential meanings that premodern interpreters knew to reside in the biblical text."[19]

What Davis honors is what I have tried to do in preaching and in this book: to view the text "through the lens of the Christian tradition of theology and liturgy." The text is the canonical text, not one that might conceivably be imagined somewhere behind it. The tradition—literally, what has been "handed on"—is a living tradition. "Finally, the mystery of

---

15. Frei, *Theology and Narrative*, 243.
16. Frei, *Theology and Narrative*, 644.
17. Green, *Imagining Theology*, 83 (citing Frei, *Theology and Narrative*).
18. Green, *Imagining Theology*, 84.
19. Davis, *Wondrous Depth*, 66.

Introduction

Christ's presence will be meaningful to faith through word and sacrament in the church."[20]

> Let us give thanks to the Lord our God.
> *It is right to give our thanks and praise!*

---

20. Frei, *Theology and Narrative*, 255.

1

The Challenge of Preaching in a Post-Establishment Church

A Confusing Time

PREACHING MATTERS; AND WORSHIP MATTERS. In the weekly assembly, we rehearse the life-saving skills of praise and thanksgiving that also support, strengthen, console, and nourish us in the Christian hope for an ultimate cosmic redemption, as it is artfully represented in word and sacrament. Unless it isn't.

A group of pastors, all members of the same denomination, were engaged in a weekly meeting focused on preaching. One of them asked the person leading the group if it were possible for pastors to devote less attention to preaching, since it could consume a lot of time—especially when a pastor's interests and strengths lay in another direction, such as counseling or community organizing. In a different setting, when a group of lay people from a downtown congregation met to share perspectives about their church's mission, one of them wondered aloud whether preaching really served a purpose any more.

As one who spent many years as a pastor, in which preparing to preach every week was the lifeline that encouraged my faith and sustained me both personally and in the work of ministry, and then joined a theological faculty as part of a team teaching both preaching and worship, such questions are startling. Had I been so sheltered that I hadn't realized that the jokes about preaching and preachers were not made lightly, for fun, but were actually serious commentary on people's experience of preaching? Had I been mistaken in believing that preaching could actually have the effect of helping to build up a congregation?

When I exchanged a pulpit for a classroom podium, it meant that my vocation shifted from preaching every Sunday to, most often, sitting in a pew among those listening to sermons rather than preaching them. The new perspective proved to be rather more different than I might have expected. Already I had discovered that preaching and pastoral care are closely linked. The one who preaches needs to be in touch with the experience and emotional lives of people who will be listening to the sermon—but not only *their* lives. A friend remarked, "I've never heard a good preacher who didn't read a lot of fiction." Why? Because fiction allows the preacher to listen in to what people are saying when they don't know a preacher is within earshot. And a novel not only pays attention to what the characters are saying, but even what they are thinking! The reader overhears what the writers of fiction are seeing and experiencing in a largely non-ecclesiastical world. The great likelihood is that the thinking and perceptions of people in congregations are not so very distant from many characters so openly revealed in the work of novelists. To preach effectively requires having listened carefully, especially to discover where the obstacles are.

The Context of Preaching

The environment in which one hears a sermon has a bigger effect on the hearer than the one in the pulpit may imagine. After a time sitting in the pews, I found that the more physically distant the listener is from the pulpit, the easier and more likely it is to hear the sermon critically. The fewer people in the congregation with whom one is at least somewhat familiar, or who have offered some welcoming gesture, the more one may feel an unintentional distancing that poses a kind of challenge to the preacher's hope of being heard.

In the COVID-19 pandemic, when we became accustomed to livestreamed "virtual" worship, the context in which one heard a sermon changed dramatically, drawing attention once again to how important a physical context is. People other than one's own family are missing, the ambiance of a space devoted to worship is lost, music heard on the laptop is experienced differently than in person. A streamed service may be experienced as a version of all the other videos that one may see online, including those one encounters unintentionally, and it competes with entertainment and sales pitches one normally finds on a screen. It is likely to feel artificial, reduced, distant, less persistently requiring our attention than is our need for another cup of coffee or to respond to a text. Even the close-up of the preacher on the screen can seem too much, the in-your-face visual distracting from the message. All these obstacles can be overcome to a point, perhaps, by unusually skillful preaching, but context matters to both the hearers and the preacher.

Context is larger than one might imagine. Context includes the emotional and intellectual environments that describe whole societies. Painting Western social and intellectual history with a wide brush, one notices that what was once easily described as "Christendom," in which faith had all the advantages of authority and popular support, lost ground during certain periods in which those advantages faded. The unquestioned authority of Christendom eventually gave way after a series of social and intellectual movements posed challenges, whether by a "renaissance" or even a "reformation," and particularly in the form of their most enduring legacy, the so-called "enlightenment." In retrospect, at least, this changed and changing environment evolved into what can be broadly described under the category of secularization.[1] Institutions and traditions that had in ages past been taken as authoritative have not only been subjected to bolder and increasingly relentless questioning, but by the twenty-first century, they appear to be on the team that's playing defense.

In the US, the losses that have been compounding under the shorthand rubric of secularization were put on pause during World War II and particularly the Cold War that followed it, during which it proved useful to counter Communist "godlessness" with democratic/free market "godliness." A whole generation grew up without much awareness of the modern challenges to faith (except perhaps as they were observable in European nations with their established churches) until the Cold War ended and "godliness" no longer served any useful political purpose. Now, as pre-WWII secularization has regained momentum in the US accompanied by even newer forms of cultural change, the generation shaped by the Cold War era may feel themselves taken by surprise. What has happened?

---

1. Taylor, *Secular Age*; and Smith, *How (Not) to Be Secular*.

The Challenge of Preaching in a Post-Establishment Church

Where Did We Go Wrong?

What has happened is that secularization is being driven on recurrent waves of social change linked to and motivated by distrust of institutions. The new social consensus suggests that each individual is autonomous, self-creating and self-defining. "Secularization," of course, is a kind of generic description of a medley of social influences interrelated and complex, new and old. The term is fuzzy enough to cover disparate phenomena from serious intellectual movements to elements of popular culture. But, whether it is possible to categorize them or not, we can no longer afford the luxury of simply ignoring the depth of these challenges or defensively denouncing newly privileged worldviews.

Fundamentalists counter secularization with claims of biblical infallibility; skeptics counter fundamentalisms with a rationalist version of infallibility tuned to the enlightenment. Many Americans, seeking to be "spiritual" but suspicious of traditional institutions as well as of tradition as such, design or patch together a personal spirituality that suits their perceived unique identity, or perhaps a series of such identities over time. The so-called "mainline" Protestant churches (the denominations that have been familiar in the US since colonial times, for the most part) find themselves challenged to learn how to talk about faith with those who have been formed in this new culture, but many whose work it is to be advocates for the gospel have discovered that even to attempt such a thing is both difficult and risky. What seemed to work well enough when establishment Protestantism was presumed to have been absorbed from the culture from birth does not seem to work in a post-establishment era.

In a technological universe in which it is easy to sample sermons online if one is inclined, it is not so terribly uncommon for the dabbler to wonder whether this or that preacher has lost confidence in the deeper and more challenging affirmations of the gospel, perhaps because doctrine seems to have been distorted or corrupted by fundamentalists who, to a surprising extent, have joined themselves hip-to-hip with right-wing politics. For example, Peter Wehner has observed that, "Perhaps without quite knowing it, many of those who most loudly proclaim the 'pre-eminence of Christ' have turned him into a means to an end, a cruel, ugly and unforgiving end. And this, too, is not quite what Jesus had in mind."[2]

---

2. Wehner, "Will Christian America Withstand," para. 17.

Easier, then, under the circumstances, for the mainline Protestant preacher to fulfill one's weekly preaching duty by focusing on whichever of the affirmations from a scriptural text are more or less congenial to whatever popular ethical consensus is prevailing, rather than wade into the deep waters that a theological engagement with the text might actually require. (This is presuming that the preacher's responsibility includes engaging deeply with Scripture in the creation of the sermon—a presumption not, evidently, beyond questioning.) It gets harder to be confident that sermons will not follow the easier way, morphing into something like motivational speaking, finding its tone in moralizing rather than taking the risk of theologizing.

On the Defensive

Of course, in an epoch in which the public is exposed day and night to all sorts of input to which we are drawn almost compulsively by means of communication devices large and small, preaching is no longer the one place where the average person is likely to be exposed to serious thought or reflection on the state of the world, the puzzling dilemmas of this mortal life, and maybe even on a wide-angle perspective that is cosmic in its scale. The preacher is competing with media both public and private characterized by ubiquitous and very confident interpretations of how things are and how they ought to be. In a culture in which a conventional version of enlightenment rationalism competes with conspiracy theories and an anti-intellectual diet of "alternative facts," most of those who preach do not feel adequately prepared to address congregations who feel certain only about politics, many of whom bring with them not much more than a kind of minimal and/or indirect acquaintance with serious Christian teaching. Those in pews as well as those in pulpits have maximal exposure to the popular consensus, including all sorts of critiques of faith, some thoughtful and some not so much.

By the last decades of the twentieth-century, the mainstream media had lost their squeamishness about drawing attention to scandals likely to embarrass the church. There are no lack of stories worthy of attention: sexual abuse, particularly but not exclusively by priests; megachurches founded and run by charismatic figures whose lives and nearly unchecked authority invite exposés; preachers of a "prosperity gospel," who exhibit personal prosperity with the help of their loyal and generous constituents;

evangelical figures of the sort who espouse a gospel linked to what at least one observer has called "toxic masculinity."[3] Once religious institutions became acceptable targets for public scrutiny, both fiction[4] and scholarship[5] began to draw attention to historical sins of the churches, both real and imagined, pre- and post-Reformation, including those in which church and state teamed up and used their combined power to punish, exclude, make war, and/or elevate one race, gender, or class at the expense of others.

While there is more to the story than is evident in the recital of these accumulated sins, the churches ought not expect to be let off the hook any more than any other institution should be. Remorse for sins, confession, and penitence are necessary always and in every circumstance, now and forever, and certainly by the church. No endeavor that is composed of and led by human beings can possibly be exempt. Contemporary ecclesiastical sins lend authority to rightful complaints as well as to moral posturing that emerges when history is viewed only through a determinedly critical lens.

Christian Faith's Influence on "Secular" Values

In fact, the churches themselves, even though often guilty as charged, have at the same time contributed to the very convictions and impulses that have shaped the liberal mind and fueled the critical judgments too easily supposed to have derived from presumably "secular" sources. The modern consensus owes more to Christian influence than is likely to be realized. One scholar has written that the unique or nearly unique features that characterized early Christianity have "become (especially for many people in the Western world) . . . commonplace."[6] In other words, what are presumed to be secular values did not all begin as secular. For example, Christianity taught what began as a specifically religious imperative to offer charitable service to others. Rodney Stark says that pagan philosophy "regarded mercy and pity as pathological emotions—defects of character to be avoided by all rational [people] . . . a defect of character unworthy of the wise."[7] Conscience, after all, in regard to its particular contents, is to a great

---

3. Du Mez, *Jesus and John Wayne*.
4. E.g., Dan Brown.
5. The atheist writers Sam Harris, Richard Dawkins, Daniel Dennett, and Christopher Hitchens.
6. Hurtado, *Destroyer of the Gods*, xi.
7. Stark, *Rise of Christianity*, 37.

> extent a cultural artifact, a historical contingency, and all of us today in the West, in some degree or another, have inherited a conscience formed by Christian moral ideals. For this reason, it is all but impossible for us to recover any real sense of the scandal that many pagans naturally felt at the bizarre prodigality with which the early Christians were willing to grant full humanity to persons of every class and condition, and of either sex.[8]

Christianity led to a softening of intimidating lines that had marked formidable divisions, such as between Jew and gentile, male and female, slave and free.

One may consider, as well, that

> despite all our vague talk of ancient or medieval "science," pagan, Muslim, or Christian, what we mean today by science—its methods, its controls and guiding principles, its desire to unite theory to empirical discovery, its trust in a unified set of physical laws, and so on—came into existence, for whatever reasons, and for better or worse, only within Christendom, and under the hands of believing Christians.[9]

But even the most familiar culturally sanctioned values need to be reevaluated occasionally. Not all retain their value over time. Individuality is important, of course, and plays a role in Christian faith, and the Reformation contributed to its rise as a counter to authoritarian, top-down conformism. However, even a good thing can be pushed too far. Individualism can undermine any confidence in or loyalty to communities, as though a community is likely to be a collective that cannot be trusted. For example, in its several versions, revivalism and churches that have been shaped by the revival mentality have often disparaged classical ways of Christian formation, focusing their attention on making individual converts, one by one, who must make a "decision for Christ." As important as personal commitment may be, labeling it as a discrete "decision" risks oversimplification. It implies that each person independently creates a kind of self-made spiritual identity fueled by personal choice, as though we live in an individualistic vacuum. It presumes that, to be genuine, faith always marks a deliberate break with one's past. In today's dominant culture, it implies that formational experiences rooted in the context of the actual life of specific communities don't count.

---

8. Hart, *Atheist Delusions*, 169.
9. Hart, *Atheist Delusions*, 169.

In mainline churches, this kind of individualism has taken the form, in effect, of breaking down the gathered church into the sum of its parts. The sense of being members of one another gets lost in the presumed supremacy of the autonomous individual, each with a potential veto. Almost every person present in the service brings to the assembly personally crafted beliefs and tastes, often feeling entitled to hear them either reinforced or at least not disturbed by either the sermon or the liturgy. Those who preach in such a way as to respect basic elements of the church's faith as represented in liturgy and sermon run the risk of emptying seats in the pews.

Can Preaching Be Taught?

Those who are responsible for teaching homiletics sometimes debate whether one can actually teach preaching. It is certain that one can teach techniques that may strengthen preaching. It helps to ponder how to begin a sermon, and how to end it. It helps to consider how one might structure the sermon so that the beginning actually leads, step by step, toward a conclusion. "Technique" includes considering a repertoire of classic rhetorical moves that may prove useful, including, of course, what we once called "illustrations": i.e., an image or story that embodies a "point" or enlivens an image; or how to make use of metaphoric/poetic/lyrical/emotionally sensitive language along with and other than a series of declarative sentences. And, naturally, the preacher needs to be able to know hearers and the culture in which they are immersed well enough to imagine how they might actually be "hearing" a sermon.

A sermon is not a lecture, not motivational speaking, not an argument, not just "happy talk," nor is it meant to be a form of manipulation or propaganda. It is, in fact, a genre of its own, not limited to description in terms of any other category of communication even though it overlaps many of them. Often, a beginning course in preaching will start by attempting to help students identify what the purposes of preaching may be. Having a purpose in mind is vital to the work of crafting a sermon in both content and method. The question of purpose is an absolutely crucial one, both in general and in specific situations. And yet it is precisely this question that one might imagine could be easily answered that is in fact most challenging.

Those who teach preaching may presume that students are more spiritually developed than in fact they may be, and so the question of the purpose of preaching may be one they are not ready to engage with any depth. And/or, students may presume that "purpose" is a silly question! They have already experienced being in worship and hearing sermons, and so they may presume that the purpose of preaching is whatever they have perceived to be the purpose of those whose preaching they have heard, or half-heard, or presumed to have heard. Yet again, if they have heard only a few sermons, they may presume that the model for preaching is something like a classroom lecture, a form familiar from their undergraduate days. From their homiletics teacher, they are eager to get on with it: "Tell us how to do it!"

One can learn technique in class, but beyond that, technique is meant to serve a purpose. More than anything else, it is necessary to have a sense of what that purpose—or mission—is. Even when some sense of the purpose and function of preaching has been personally grasped, most preachers have to teach themselves how to realize that mission by their own experience in a pulpit—otherwise said, by trial and error. From my own experience, I am persuaded that if preachers have a passion to communicate, they will find a way to do it, even if their technique doesn't follow the rules in the book.

Passion

What do I mean by passion? Passion is not yelling and exhorting; not getting all worked up. Passion involves a personal investment, a sense that what we are dealing with in preaching matters, and that it matters to the preacher personally as well as professionally. But, why should it matter? To use biblical as well as homiletical language, it matters because it has to do with salvation, that of the preachers as well as those to whom they are preaching.

Granted, "salvation" covers a lot of territory, and is not to be defined simplistically, as though its alternative were inevitably damnation! I choose the word cautiously, because it risks being misunderstood. But it seems a necessary choice, if only because it deals with the existential, possesses a character of urgency, as though once glimpsed, however dimly, it is impossible to turn one's eyes away indifferently. In short, it is personal (not the same as private), and has relational dimensions that run deep and are something other than simply a collection of opinions or suggestions.

Passion cannot be taught, although mentors can help to strengthen it once it has been caught. A passion to communicate results when the preacher discovers the awesomeness of that place suspended between the scriptural text and a congregation who, like the preacher, find themselves in a fast-moving world that constantly presents its challenges: intellectual challenges, sure; but also social and political challenges, as well as some that are deeply personal. The ancient text embodies, in a variety of ways of using language, some sense of a transcendent word, a word from God, spoken through the writers for hearers in a particular time and place.

But even though that word was first spoken to people of other places and times than our own, it can also be heard, with help of the Holy Spirit, as it becomes a contemporary word for our generation and for countless other generations to hear and to follow. The key is to listen in hope of hearing that divine word as a dynamic one that is meant to engage us in our own context even now. The power of Scripture should not be underestimated. It has demonstrated the ability to capture the imaginations of people from all classes and cultures, bringing with them varying degrees of sophistication, for many generations including even our own.

That word, God reaching out to us, nearly always has some ethical or moral dimension. At least, one can extrapolate from a text some clue to a personal or social imperative. But, the text in its larger scriptural context is always theologically rooted. In the era in which we are living, the theological is often under suspicion, sometimes because of ways God-talk has been abused, and partly because we find it difficult to trust or believe in any authority whatsoever, but particularly any authority that cannot be fully explained in a way sufficient to eliminate all doubt. So, it becomes easy to highlight the ethical and minimize the theological. A problem is that congregations can hear discourses almost anywhere about how to be "good" people both personally and socially. One can also encounter such imperatives while reading the *Washington Post*, the *New York Times*, or even *Reader's Digest*. And, because success in becoming a "good" person is hard to evaluate objectively, hearing about our personal and social obligations can either make it too easy for us to congratulate ourselves on our virtue, or on the other hand, to discourage and wear us out. Scripture—both testaments—links theology and ethics as two movements in the same symphony.

Preaching the Difficult Texts

In my own experience sitting in that space between Scripture and the tumble of the world, it seems as though the most rewarding sermons tend to be those based on the most difficult texts, including, yes: miracles, exorcisms, death and resurrection, ascension, judgment, a new heaven and earth. Perhaps they are often most rewarding because they require the deepest dives into the text, the most artful wrestling with how to perceive and understand these things both in themselves and as they might touch the lives of people in contemporary society. Texts that seem easier because they focus on values that seem to be conventionally popular, such as love, inclusiveness, and generosity can seduce us into engaging them too simply.

Rarely are they simple. To engage them in their scriptural context requires recognizing their indebtedness to a sense of God's character and disposition towards us that are rooted in precisely those difficult "miracle" texts, the kind that come to life when the preacher is personally engaged rather than just repeating the words in a Bible commentary. It is, after all, God's character and disposition towards us that describe and support a credible way of understanding what matters in this confused and confusing world. And not only what matters, but where our support comes from. It has felt urgent to think my way through these challenges not just because the preacher is supposed to stand up and say something at least once a week, but because they matter to me and my sense of myself and my place in the world. Because they matter to me, I learn to struggle to find a way to communicate to others *why* they matter. Ethics, morality, politics, theology are all wrapped together in the struggle to hear what the Holy One is saying.

That blend should be pondered when one is learning to preach or when assisting a search committee looking for a pastor. Congregational surveys tell pastoral search committees that they should look for someone who is a "good" preacher. The challenge is that more often than not, neither those who ask for a "good" preacher nor the search committee has a clear idea about how to describe what a "good" preacher might be. The bar of expectations has been set low. Sometimes it is simply enough that the preacher produce a sermon that one can actually listen to all the way through. Sometimes it will have to do with political compatibility, or sense of humor, or with not expecting much work on the part of listeners. A shirttail relative was in a congregation who had recently installed a new pastor. Asked about him, she described the new pastor, generously, as preaching "practical little sermons." Practical. Little. Not much effort required by the congregation.

It would seem to be nearly impossible to compare preaching in one era with preaching in another. Of course, in some periods congregations have been more prepared, more receptive, and more likely to credit the preacher as speaking authoritatively than in other eras. Impressionistic evaluations of preaching in our time would suggest that, broadly speaking, sermons might more realistically be described as making do in an era of transition. If that is the case, one might speculate that making do is what we do when we don't really know what to do. And we don't really know what to do because the challenges we face are complex and not easily engaged all at once, and our congregations bring with them every aspect of this complexity, most encountered every day, even every few minutes while checking their electronic devices, quite apart from the complexity of lived experience. The preacher's best strategy may be to stick with the familiar, or at least not to rock the boat. But the boat is already rocking.

A Transitional Moment

As Christendom recedes, being replaced by a configuration that is not yet clear to us, we find ourselves in a transitional moment. Things are not what they used to be, nor are they yet what they are going to be. However, it feels safe to say that this transitional status presses us toward what might be perceived as two choices: save the institution at all costs, or preach the gospel for its own sake, however things may turn out for the institution. Granted, this may not be a choice that one makes entirely consciously or decisively, but it is a choice recognizable from a distance just by observing the various ways that preaching responds to the pressures of the day.

For example, when preaching minimizes what I am calling the "challenging parts," replacing, say, cross and resurrection with therapies, or political imperatives, or strategies for "successful" living, the choice apparently being made is to save the institution. This choice does not necessarily mean giving up on Jesus, because he is, after all, an effective teacher, and people expect to hear something from him in church. But it does mean deciding not to say much about Jesus *Christ*, in whom God is self-revealing, and whose revealing is effected not in teaching alone, but in teaching that was lived out in an embodied way in both cross and resurrection. So, the second option is to preach those central things—incarnation, ministry, cross, resurrection, ascension, coming again—difficult as they are in any era, but posing particular challenges in our own. This choice may possibly require bracing oneself should it lead to losing the filled pews of blessed memory, if that is what has to be for the gospel's sake. Nadia Bolz-Weber states the case clearly:

> But the job of a preacher is to find some kind of good news for people. And that good news really should be about who God is and how God works and what God has done and what God will do. (What passes for preaching in many cases is more "here's the problem, and here's what you can do about it," which I myself have never once heard as being "good news.")[10]

Those preachers who feel themselves pressed daily to share the default skepticism of our age may not be able to resist following wherever the crowds are going. Within memory, crowds were attracted to churches for various reasons: respectability, moral and ethical reflection, networking, community, doing good works, exposure to the arts (in some cases), or programming for children, and yes, of course, to express and nurture faith. But, although marketing successes have been perceived to be normal for the church since the time of Constantine, the church of Jesus Christ can not only exist but also persist even when numbers are smaller. Further, those who remain loyal to gospel and church may find that lifting up the central things, the "challenging parts," attracts some who are not content with conforming to the dominant culture and submitting to its presumed authority without questioning it. In other words, there will always be some who will wonder if there could be an alternative to the status quo. They may be attracted to Buddhism, to Islam, to evangelicalism, or even to a church that is shaped by solid theology with a strongly sacramental dimension, one led by its theology to be open to the world.

Learning from Mom and Dad

When I first began preaching, it helped me to try to visualize my own parents in the pews. Both my father and my mother were uncomfortable with religious faith as they knew it. I don't know the whole of their separate stories, but my father seems to have had little or no systematic Christian formation, and my mother felt oppressed by a father who had become

---

10. Bolz-Weber, *Pastrix*, 56.

obsessed with a new pietistic faith for which he had left behind his mainstream Methodism. In any case, we had a church in our community with which the family had distant but historic ancestral connections, but it was a church we were consistent in approaching only occasionally.

Newly ordained and trying to learn to preach, both parents helped me, although they did not know that they did. Was it just my luck? Or was it providential? They helped me to be free of the illusion that everyone hearing me preach was already a believer, loyal to the church and its faith, and knowledgeable about it. I could have learned that in other ways, particularly since I have always been a relentless reader, including a lot of fiction. But it was more real to me because I knew that my parents were good people, decent people, people who might very well have been regulars at church, but chose not to be. Many folks not so very different from them were in the pews, though. It was not enough just to say, "Believe this, because it's in the Bible," or "Christ died for our sins," or "We are saved by grace." Even for those who are accustomed to hearing those words or just not interested enough to object to them need to find a point of personal access before they are likely to feel inclined to consider taking them to heart.

Having begun as a preacher with the awareness that the pews were filled with people who were not necessarily hostile, but dealing with skepticism in one way or another, it shaped what I brought to preaching. But it also helped me to recognize my own skepticism, those parts of me that were never content just to take for granted what I had not wrestled with myself. As society has increasingly come to trust skepticism more than it trusts what it perceives to be the message of the church, I am more and more grateful for the school of skepticism that prepared me for a preaching ministry, particularly in these post-establishment times.

2

Preaching What Is Prayed
The Renewal of All Things

Finding Our Path

AT THE CENTER OF PRE-REFORMATION worship was the sacrament, the Lord's Supper, the Eucharist, celebrated every Sunday and, in fact, nearly every day, more often than not with no more than a single communicant, the priest himself. Preaching, however, was more often occasional. The Reformers recognized that the marginalization of preaching, and particularly the near absence of preaching that engaged deeply and personally with a biblical text, in effect consented to the distortion of the sacrament. It may be that "consented" is not strong enough: "contributed to" may be more accurate. So, to recover preaching alongside the sacrament was a move toward the recovery of a Eucharist both more accessible and more closely attuned to the narrative at the center of Christian faith.

And yet, although the reforms were important, in the long run, practice turned out differently from what Luther or Calvin expected. Post-Reformation, word and sacrament again became divided, just in a different way. After the Reformation, sooner and later the norm became preaching every Sunday, but celebrating the Eucharist only periodically. If the near absence of preaching contributes to a distortion of the sacrament, is it not possible that the near absence of the sacrament may contribute to a distortion of preaching? "A church that loses the Word must finally lose the

Sacrament. But is it not equally true that a church which loses the Sacrament must finally lose the Word?"[1]

Miroslav Volf, who teaches theology at Yale Divinity School, came to believe that the Eucharist serves to strengthen preaching. At least, it can serve to hold preaching accountable. Volf was "disturbed by the failure of many preachers to make the center of the Christian faith the center of their proclamation." Of course, as Volf notes, it is unfortunately the case that some ministers "feel as entitled to redesign the Sacraments as they feel inclined to avoid the cross of Christ. But where the Sacraments are left intact, they point straight back to Christ's self-giving on the cross."[2] The eucharistic prayer points to the central affirmations of the Christian gospel realized in the person of Jesus Christ, his ministry of healing and exorcism, his cross and resurrection, his ascension and promise to come again. In him and his story, set in the context of Israel's story and expectations, we encounter what otherwise we would not know: God's character and disposition towards us, and the breadth and grandeur of the redemption promised. When these biblical testimonies are rehearsed and revisited in the words and actions of the Eucharist, they may gently guide preachers to lift up the same affirmations in the biblical texts to which they are accountable in their preaching.

But notice the caveat here. And in fact there are two caveats. One is that Volf has discovered by experience that there are occasions in which, indeed, the presiding minister may imagine that the job description provides discretion to "redesign the sacraments" for some "good" reason or other.

The second caveat is that the presiding minister may be in a church in which it is normal to improvise even the sacraments, or, perhaps the church has guidelines for sacramental celebrations, but ministers are not really held responsible should they not pay much attention to them. Both of these caveats describe what is actually in play across the spectrum of several denominations. In such cases, even an improvised Eucharist in its rightful place next to the sermon may not be able to embody its message forcefully enough to guide and direct the preacher of the word of God to what Volf rightfully calls "the center of the Christian faith."

---

1. Hageman, *Pulpit and Table*, 115.
2. Volf, "Proclaiming the Lord's Death," 253.

"Understanding" Sacramentally

The Reformation was a movement driven at least in part by the need for the ordinary Christian to *understand* the substance of the faith well enough to be genuinely nourished and formed by it—in other words, to experience preaching, for example, sacramentally, as an occasion in which God might be expected to make the divine presence known. The same impulse led to moves toward the recovery and renewal of the Eucharist. The Reformation passion for *understanding* is best understood as an experiential aspiration as much as an intellectual one. However, the Renaissance and Reformation passion for understanding was eventually overtaken by the Enlightenment version, with its optimistic ambition of being guided solely by "pure reason."

New York Times columnist David Brooks has written about research that studies how the brain works, and it does not work the way we think it does, nor is reason as distinct from emotion as we have liked to believe.

> It feels as if the rational brain creates and works with ideas, but that emotions sweep over us. But some neuroscientists, like Lisa Feldman Barrett of Northeastern University, argue that people construct emotions and thoughts, and there is no clear distinction between them. It feels as if we can use our faculty of reason to restrain our passions, but some neuroscientists doubt this is really what's happening. Furthermore, emotions assign value to things, so they are instrumental to reason, not separate from or opposed to it.[3]

The Enlightenment has become the very air we all breathe, and its triumph is celebrated by those in the know and its influence felt by them and all the rest of us. So now, in the twenty-first century, our situation has changed. We (in so-called "mainline" churches) find ourselves not only to have taken to heart the need to *understand* the gospel, but to understand it in ways congenial to and acceptable to the enlightened. One soon discovers the limits of "understanding." The sophisticated but naïve belief that there is such a thing as "pure reason" leaves no room for either the cross or resurrection, not to mention the *basileia*. The requirements for objective evidence and rational explanation nearly incapacitate us from embracing a necessary mystery.

Andrew Louth observes that the life, death, and resurrection of Jesus Christ disclose to us "the true character of mystery: mystery not just as the

---

3. Brooks, "You Are Not," 23.

focus for *our* questioning and investigating, but mystery as that which *questions us*, which calls us to account."[4] Encounter with this mystery leads to a kind of "knowing" that overflows the capacity for explanation. Rationality becomes irrational when it rules out all experience that cannot be reduced to a kind of pseudo-mathematical precision.

Could it be that in this new era it may be the Eucharist that both draws us holistically into the mystery of the gospel, and teaches us how to preach from "the center of the Christian faith"? Karl Barth wrote that "Preaching, in fact, derives its substance from the sacrament which itself refers to an action in the total event of revelation. Preaching is a commentary on and an interpretation of the sacrament, having the same meaning but in words."[5] It is, of course, always possible to avoid the road less traveled, even when it leads us to where we need to go. But the way has been opened if we are willing to dare it. The sacramental meal can lead us to risk preaching that theologizes, wrestles with the living God, listens for a word that comes from God, as we deliberately and intentionally follow the eucharistic lead.

Recovering an Eschatological Imagination

My own theology was reshaped years after seminary by my introduction to the riches of the Great Thanksgiving, another name for eucharistic prayer. If such prayer was taught during my years acquiring the MDiv, I did not encounter it. That is not so very unusual for those serving or preparing to serve in Protestant denominations other than Lutheran or Episcopal (if Episcopalians permit me to identify them as Protestants). It is true that my own Presbyterian denomination (PCUSA) and its Scottish and continental kin had experienced the beginnings of exploring historically where and how liturgical practice and theology intersect as early as at least the mid-nineteenth century, and other confessions were moving in the same direction as well. Such explorations paralleled a similar one in the Roman Catholic Church. However, it was the Second Vatican Council (1962–65) that brought issues related to worship into the sunlight for all to see. The Council validated changes in Roman Catholic liturgy that paralleled, in some instances, the reforms—or desired reforms—of the sixteenth century.

For example, the language. Post-Vatican II, the Mass would from here on be celebrated (almost always) in the vernacular. Catholics actually

4. Davis, *Wondrous Depth*, 7–8.
5. Barth, *Preaching of the Gospel*, 23.

began introducing changes that seemed enormous even in the 1960s, and their reforms lent some courage to cautious Protestants, who would soon enough manage to give up the King James Bible's "thees" and "thous" that had characterized Protestant prayer for generations. Small changes, these, but they were followed by engaging far more serious matters, including the character of the sacraments. By the 1960s, denominations that were updating worship guidelines and service books already had available to them a wealth of liturgical scholarship, both old and new.

New liturgical texts appeared for celebrating the sacraments, both Baptism and the Lord's Supper. The newer forms were not always radically different from what was already available in existing service books, but in most cases, the older forms minimized or even entirely ignored the eschatological promise that might be described as a "renewal of all things" (Matt 19:28). The newer prayers draw attention to emerging ecumenical norms that lift up the eschatological horizons that could easily go unnoticed until one is led to pay attention to them. Those who pray the new eucharistic prayers would find it hard to miss the Memorial Acclamation, in which the assembly sings "Christ has died, Christ is risen, Christ will come again," or alternative acclamations equally direct.

The publication of a whole new Presbyterian *Book of Common Worship* as early as 1993 provided easy access to a kind of users' guide that explained the form and contents of the Great Thanksgiving for those who might choose to pray it without a written text.[6] I confess that, in my uninstructed naiveté, it had not occurred to me that there might be expectations of a specific form and content in eucharistic prayer, other than use of the words of institution.

What began to strike me most forcefully were the eschatological references in the new prayers as, for example, in the 1964 pamphlet describing the proposed Presbyterian *Service for the Lord's Day*. These eschatological references are too subtle, but notable nevertheless. The first follows the words of institution when they are included in the body of the prayer rather than in a warrant preceding it. "Remembering the Lord Jesus Christ, we take this bread and this cup, proclaiming his death for the sins of the world, and confessing his resurrection *until he comes again*."[7] Of course, "until he comes" is biblical language, following the Pauline wording of the

---

6. Presbyterian Church (USA), "Great Thanksgiving J," 156.

7. Presbyterian Church (USA), *Service for the Lord's Day*, 22. (Italics here and following by the author.)

institution narrative from 1 Cor 11:26 with the addition of "again," while differing from the words of institution used in both the Roman Canon and in Luther's liturgy, which, in both cases, combine aspects from the synoptic Gospels and I Corinthians without the words "until he comes." The second and more striking reference in the 1964 proposed *Service for the Lord's Day* is in the *epiclesis*, the prayer for the Holy Spirit.

> Grant, O Lord, that thy Holy Spirit may come among us; that the bread we break and the cup we share may be for us a means of grace; that, receiving them, we may be made one with Christ and he with us, and remain faithful members of his body *until we feast with him anew in his Kingdom.*[8]

In the same year, 1964, the United Church of Christ published a similar pamphlet with its proposed *Lord's Day Service* including thanksgiving for Jesus Christ "who rules over us Lord above all, prays for us continually, and *will return again in triumph.*" The *epiclesis* in this service includes a petition that we may remain faithful members of his body *until we feast with him anew in thy heavenly kingdom."*[9]

Similarly, the Episcopal Church approved a new *Book of Common Prayer* in 1979. In Rite II of *Holy Eucharist*, a petition in the Great Thanksgiving prays that the Holy Spirit will "*at the last day bring us with all your saints into the joy of your eternal kingdom.*"[10]

Other denominations exhibit similar additions in the new liturgies and service books of the last third of the twentieth century, an indicator of a wider movement toward the recovery of eschatology so evident in the Bible, both testaments, but sidelined for centuries. Historically, reference to the coming of God's kingdom (*basileia*, in New Testament Greek) is relatively rare even in the older eucharistic prayers for which we have texts. However, the very earliest is found in the *Didache*, from the first century, possibly around 60 CE.

> Remember, Lord, your Church, to deliver it from all evil and to perfect it in your love; bring it together from the four winds, now sanctified, *into your kingdom which you have prepared for it.*[11]

---

8. Presbyterian Church (USA), *Service for the Lord's Day.*
9. United Church of Christ. *The Lord's Day Service*, 17.
10. Episcopal Church, *Book of Common Prayer*, 363.
11. Jasper and Cuming, *Prayers of the Eucharist*, 24.

Following shortly after in this prayer is the Greek *"Marana tha,"* translated by the early Greek doctors of the church as "The Lord has come," but "should probably be translated '*Come, Lord,*' as in . . . I Corinthians 16:22."[12]

A Gift from the East

For a long time, early Christian eucharistic prayers followed generally shared guidelines but were not written down, so it is possible, even likely, that presiders prayed *ex tempore* for the coming of the *basileia* at least sometimes over the centuries before we begin to see such prayers in examples of ancient written texts. In any case, it is in the Eastern church where one can find prayers at Eucharist that foresee and anticipate the reign of God, the new creation, or, as Jesus put it at least once, "the renewal of all things." "Truly I tell you, at *the renewal of all things*, when the Son of Man is seated on the throne of his glory, you who have followed me will also sit on twelve thrones, judging the tribes of Israel" (Matt 19:28). One Orthodox example would be from The Liturgy of St. James, about 451 CE, in which the prayer recalls Christ's death, resurrection, ascension, *"and his glorious and awesome second coming, when he comes with glory to judge the living and the dead."*[13] Except, perhaps, for some of the several Gallican rites in the Western church, influenced by the Eastern church in an era in which absolute uniformity was not consistently enforced in the church of Rome, churches under papal jurisdiction likely knew nothing of prayer for the coming of the *basileia*. It is not present in the Roman Canon, which "acquired its form between the end of the fourth century and the seventh century, and has not been changed significantly since the days of Pope Gregory the Great (d. 604)."[14]

In any case, the priest prayed the Canon *sotto voce*, so that it could not have been heard even if anyone listening understood Latin. The Canon was the prayer of the Roman See, and would have been in use in the jurisdictions known to Luther and Calvin. Neither of these Reformers' eucharistic prayers as such included an eschatological petition either, although Calvin included something like it in the intercessions:

---

12. Jasper and Cuming, *Prayers of the Eucharist*, 24. In the NRSV, "Our Lord, come!"
13. Jasper and Cuming, *Prayers of the Eucharist*, 92.
14. Mazza, *Eucharistic Prayers*, 53.

> And thus may every power and principality which stands against
> thy glory be destroyed and abolished day by day, *till the fulfillment
> of thy kingdom be manifest, when thou shalt appear in judgment.*[15]

The twentieth-century reforms of the Second Vatican Council led to the creation of three new eucharistic prayers licensed for use in the Roman Catholic Church, although the Roman Canon continues to be the first and preeminent. In Roman eucharistic prayers two, three, and four, there have been added an identical addition to the prayer: "Lord, we proclaim your death and we confess your resurrection, *until you come.*"[16] The third also prays,

> Mindful therefore, Lord, of the saving passion of your Son and
> of his wonderful resurrection and ascension into heaven, but also
> *looking forward to his second coming.*[17]

and in the fourth prayer, "we profess his resurrection and ascension to your right hand, and, *looking forward to his coming in glory.*"[18]

Why the recovery of these liturgical gestures pointing to the *parousia*, Christ's coming again? One reason is that researchers in the various confessional bodies had already been studying ancient liturgies for at least a hundred years before Vatican II. Another was the influence of the new interest in biblical studies in the twentieth century, and their impact on liturgical scholarship. All of the new prayers, Protestant and Catholic, have been influenced by the same model, the West Syrian or Antiochene model of eucharistic prayer that has historically been the primary form in the Eastern churches. The classic Liturgy of St. Basil and that of St. John Chrysostom are examples. The Orthodox churches' prayers managed to keep in liturgical memory a primary testimony of the New Testament in association with the sacramental meal, one available for recovery after generations of neglect in the West. For those who take seriously the hope of the ultimate manifestation of Christ as sovereign, bringing with him a new creation and a new heaven and earth, the new prayers following the West Syrian example point us in the right direction: a cosmic redemption (see, for example, 1 Cor 15:24; Gal 6:15; 2 Pet 3:13).

---

15. Thompson, *Liturgies of the Western Church*, 201.
16. Mazza, *Eucharistic Prayers*, 89, 129, 156.
17. Mazza, *Eucharistic Prayers*, 131.
18. Mazza, *Eucharistic Prayers*, 156.

A Taste of the Glorious Kingdom

In the classical Eastern Orthodox tradition, the Eucharist itself is understood to be "the manifestation and presence of the kingdom of God."[19] Where Christ is, the kingdom is, and just as Christ was present, for example, at the wedding in Cana, he is present to us and for us, sacramentally, in the Lord's Supper. A vision of the ultimate future, the *basileia*, may be discernible in the sacrament for those with ears to hear and eyes to see. The *basileia* is both more than and other than any direct representation of it or any possible description of it in any language. And yet, it is possible to glimpse a sign of it here and there, now and then, often in unexpected instances when it seems that justice has prevailed or that love has triumphed over hate or indifference. Scripture provides verbal clues that enable the faithful to catch the sense of the *basileia* in the sacramental meal itself, directing us toward the "wedding banquet,"[20] God's gift of a joyful fulfillment to be marked by homecoming, reunion, and reconciliation.

Alexander Schmemann, an Orthodox theologian, laments that in formal, academic theology, eschatology has typically been "virtually reduced to the doctrine of 'God as the Judge and Avenger.' As to piety, i.e., the personal experience of individual believers, the interest is narrowed to the question of one's personal fate 'after death.'"[21] In other words, the ultimate Christian hope is rather to be played out on a huge screen, certainly inclusive of individuals, but not focused on who is in and who is out. The Greek Orthodox Church of the Holy Saviour in Chora, a neighborhood of Istanbul, is now a mosque, but between 1315 and 1321 it was decorated with striking Christian mosaics. One of them is a picture of Christ, in which the Savior holds Adam by the wrist in one hand and Eve in the other, pulling them out of hell. This image of Jesus Christ "harrowing hell," sweeping up those who have been lost there and carrying them to safety, points to the ultimate eschatological hope: the redemption of the whole cosmos. It is not all that hard to get into hell, whether for a brief visit or the length of one's life, but God's intention is to pull us out.

---

19. Schmemann, *Eucharist*, 29.
20. Matt 22:1–10; 26:29, Luke 13:29; 14:15; Rev 19:9.
21. Schmemann, *Eucharist*, 42.

An apolytikion is a prayer that summarizes the liturgical occasion being celebrated for a particular day in the Orthodox liturgical calendar, such as this one for Easter by the Antiochian Orthodox Church of North America:

> When thou didst descend unto death, O Life immortal, then thou didst destroy hades with the brilliance of thy divinity; and when thou didst raise the dead from beneath the earth, all the powers of heaven did cry aloud unto thee: O Christ, thou Giver of life, glory to thee, O our God.[22]

Like the Old Testament, the New Testament includes texts that would seem to contradict each other, such as these two below. But rather than canceling each other out, they and many others like them serve as a kind of both/and, for which the best adjective is paradoxical. Each needs to be read in the light of the other. Judgment is necessary, but the judge turns out, in the end, to be gracious.

---

22. Antiochian Orthodox Christian Archdiocese of North America, *Liturgikon*, 325.

"Truly I tell you, just as you did it not to one of the least of these, you did not do it to me." And these will go away into eternal punishment, but the righteous into eternal life. (Matt 25:45–46)	For to this end we toil and struggle, because we have our hope set on the living God, who is the Savior of all people, especially of those who believe. (1 Tim 4:10)

Judgment Day?

Surely we shall not escape some kind of "judgment day." Injustices and injuries inflicted both upon us and by us upon others cannot be healed without being exposed, requiring the kind of reckoning that cannot help but be painful. But judgment and mercy are two sides of the same coin. Judgment has to do with justice; but while justice may come as a welcome relief, it is hard to take when it hits home. The good news is that the judge will be that One who has already walked in our streets. The One who is to judge has been judged himself; has been scorned and mocked by the bitter judgment of strangers, and his life discarded. The judge will be that One whose counsel it was not to look for ways to get even, but to refuse to return evil for evil. And, while Jesus made it clear that the stakes are high, and choices matter, and, somehow, consequences will be paid, he also accepted the hospitality of lost people with unsavory reputations and showed them what love looks like and how it can reshape lives. We have a judge whose intention it is to restore and redeem rather than to strike and destroy.

> Let the floods clap their hands;
>   let the hills sing together for joy
> at the presence of the Lord, for he is coming
>   to judge the earth.
> He will judge the world with righteousness,
>   and the peoples with equity. (Ps 98:8–9)

So, consider what this eschatological hope means for our relationships with people who do not match our conventional diagnoses of the kind of person who may be "in" with God. Consider what it means in the way our personal piety is shaped, and consider what it means for preaching. It seems not to be necessary to speculate on the ultimate destiny of the Hindu, the atheist, the agnostic, the family member who has given up on the whole thing, or even the justifiably disgraced. God's redemptive energy is not easily exhausted. Grace reaches further than we imagine, and is likely not stymied even by that formidable boundary that marks the frontier between this mortal life, and death. When Stephen made his testimony to Christ and the resurrection before the high priest, he was stoned to death. As he died, he prayed, "Lord, do not hold this sin against them" (Acts 7:60). Judgment is necessary and unavoidable, but even beyond rightful judgment, we may reasonably hope for mercy for the judged.

And, preachers, our anxiety about appearing to be as narrow as those who draw exclusive lines without hesitation does not have to lead us to preaching a gospel that skips over the challenging parts: the centrality of Jesus Christ, his cross and resurrection; and his call to discipleship. Jesus is not a problem to be avoided or a cause for embarrassment whom we might manage to salvage if confined to the role of a remarkable teacher. He is rather the ultimate exhibition of God's character as the One who comes looking for us in whatever lost places we may be found, and for Whom not even faithlessness, death or even hell poses an impossible obstacle. The prophet Isaiah imagined a servant who looks, in retrospect, something like Jesus.

> And now the LORD says,
> who formed me in the womb to be his servant
> ...
> "It is too light a thing that you should be my servant
> to raise up the tribes of Jacob
> and to restore the survivors of Israel;
> I will give you as a light to the nations,
> that my salvation may reach to the end of the earth." (Isa 49:5a–6)

Scripture Critiquing Scripture

In the Bible, Scripture both interprets Scripture and critiques Scripture. God more than once condemns Israel for faithlessness and indifference to both justice and mercy, and then paradoxically promises not to abandon this people. Similarly, God judges the nations relentlessly, and then asserts that they have not been written off or forgotten, but, for example, "I am coming to gather all nations and tongues; and they shall come and see my glory" (Isa 66:18).

In my first pastorate, a group was studying the parable of the laborers in the vineyard (Matt 20:1–16). A landowner needed workers, who were likely to be found in the open marketplace where those who needed a job showed up in hopes of earning enough to support their families for another day. The landowner started looking for help early in the morning, found workers available, and contracted with them to work for a day "at the usual daily wage." As the day progressed, the landowner returned to the marketplace four more times looking for workers, at 9:00 a.m., 12 noon, 3:00 p.m., and finally, at 5:00 p.m. He said to each of the four latter groups that he would pay them "whatever is right." At the end of the workday, all were paid, beginning with the last hired and ending with those hired early in the morning. When the last hired were paid what the first hired had been promised, "the usual daily wage," the first hired expected they might be paid more than had been promised; but no, they were paid exactly what had been agreed. Not surprisingly, they complained.

The group studying the parable complained, too. They called it the "terrible parable." It is true, I think, that we human beings have an inbuilt sense of justice, and pure justice would have called for being rewarded in proportion to the time and labor each group of workers had spent. The landowner had not reneged on his promise to the early comers, but his generosity seemed not to recognize the special contribution of these who had labored the longest. But our indignation may be fueled by the fact that most of us are inclined to imagine that, if we had been characters in the parable, we would surely have been among those who had labored the longest in the heat of the day, wouldn't we? But in fact, the likelihood is that we might not be able to assess with objectivity the likelihood of our being the longest and hardest workers in such a situation. We may quite as easily be among those who end up being rewarded above and beyond what we might rightfully "deserve."

My reading of the parable sees it through theological rather than economic lenses. Those who were at work longest are stand-ins for, I think, Israel, God's chosen people. Those who worked the shorter times represent the gentiles, all the other peoples of the earth. Israel's calling had been to bear the burden of "chosenness," not for special privilege but for the heavy labor of witnessing to the one God in an inhospitable environment. We gentiles are latecomers. Nevertheless, what is decisive here is God's generosity. The landowner speaks in God's place:

> "I choose to give to this last the same as I give to you. Am I not allowed to do what I choose with what belongs to me? Or are you envious because I am generous?" So the last will be first, and the first will be last. (Matt 20:14–16)

Those of us who are gentiles are the beneficiaries of God's unexpected generosity, for which Israel certainly has a greater claim. Clearly, Israel has served in the field longer. And yet, in the inclusion of the gentiles no harm has really been done to those recruited first (Israel), and in the end it does not much matter who is first or last. One may be persuaded that God's generosity is generously accorded not only to those of other than Jewish ethnicities, but even to those who never in this life will perceive or respond to God's hand or voice extended to them—i.e., really, really latecomers. If grace is really grace, then it is unbounded and unconditional, and there is no expiration date on it.

Similarly, in Luke's story of the prodigal son, the older of the two sons has been faithful to his father all along. Does he represent Israel? He has shown up every day to manage the farm while his younger brother has been a no-show. Does the younger son, who came late to appeal to his father's mercy, represent the gentiles? When the father of both joyfully celebrates the younger son's return, his older brother feels resentful. Is he a stand-in for Israel, feeling slighted by this awkward embrace of the latecomer? But the father says to him, "Son, you are always with me, and all that is mine is yours. But we had to celebrate and rejoice, because this brother of yours was dead and has come to life; he was lost and has been found" (Luke 15:11–32).

Here again the story is about generosity: about grace, to use theological language. Grace gives more than is deserved, strictly speaking. It takes nothing away from anyone else. Grace is not reasonable by conventional calculations, but it is God's way, and it is upon grace that we would do better to place our hope in the end. No one is exempt from the need for a generosity that serves to overcome our deficits. God's grace is strong enough, persistent enough to empty hell, indeed, to empty all the hells in which we will ever find ourselves. Surely it is prudent for Christians, however righteous we may judge ourselves to be, to pray for grace at least as urgently as we pray for justice. As in Israel's crossing of the Red Sea, it appears that there may be a way open for those for whom there had seemed to be no way. Jesus said,

> Then people will come from east and west, from north and south, and will eat in the kingdom of God. Indeed, some are last who will be first, and some are first who will be last. (Luke 13:28–29)

The twentieth-century theologian, Karl Barth, "replaced Calvin's double predestination—some elected to salvation, some to damnation—with *universal election of humanity to be with the Father by the Father's election of the Son to crucifixion and exaltation*."[23]

In the New Testament, Jesus healed some who clearly had faith in him beforehand, and some without faith who were brought to him by an advocate, and some who had exhibited no prior faith in him either personally or via an intercessor. For an example of the latter, consider the case of Jesus healing the woman he encountered in a synagogue on the Sabbath. Luke describes her as being a person "with a spirit that had crippled her for eighteen years." Jesus noticed her, and it was obvious that she was in distress. "When Jesus saw her, he called her over and said, 'Woman, you are set free from your ailment.' When he laid his hands on her, immediately she stood up straight and began praising God" (Luke 13:11–13). If, in Christ, God can and does reach out even to those for whom there is no evidence of prior faith, the breadth and power of divine mercy is surely not measured out grudgingly, as though there were a risk of its running out.

When we take the eschatological vision seriously, we find ourselves corrected when we have limited our attention only on "going to heaven" one by one. The church, unfortunately, at some point became embarrassed by its hope for a cosmic redemption that had come to seem so remote as not to be worthy of much attention in preaching or teaching. That led and still leads to a narrowing, a presumption that some will be included and some will be excluded, along with a readiness to identify which are which. This readiness to rule some out has become, in our own time, a temptation that has seduced some of those who preach, while, on the other hand, inducing many others, particularly "mainline" preachers, to turn away from addressing ultimate questions altogether. One can understand and sympathize; yet, our hope rests in the God of the promised *basileia*. James, reflecting on the law, judgment, and mercy, reaches the point where he must say, "mercy triumphs over judgment" (Jas 2:13b). May it be so.

---

23. Willimon, *How Odd of God*, 27; citing Barth, *Church Dogmatics* II/2, 76.

3

The Reformation
Preaching to Get Ready for Heaven

Reformation Adjustments

PROTESTANTS DID NOT INVENT PREACHING, but the Reformation brought preaching from the margins to the center. Practice was not uniform by any means in the late pre-Reformation church, varying from region to region. In some places, such as North Africa and middle Italy, only the bishop could preach, but often the bishop's jurisdiction was small enough that every little town had its bishopric. In large dioceses, restricting local priests from preaching "was quite necessary because of the none-too-high ability of the priests."[1] In other regions, such as parts of France, parish priests were allowed to preach. Or, an alternative to a sermon was to read aloud from homilies of the "fathers" of the ancient church.

> The Carolingian-Reform-Synods of 813 expressly demanded the translation of the homilies into the people's tongue. The requirements of the clergy were supplied by various collections of homilies, such as were prepared for reading at monastic choir prayer . . . or others that offered an explanation of the Epistle and Gospels.[2]

In the high Middle Ages, there occurred a revival of the sermon, but not as part of the regular liturgy. As the various religious orders emerged, they produced from among their members mission preachers who would

1. Jungmann, *Mass*, 290.
2. Jungmann, *Mass*.

itinerate from parish to parish when invited, but their preaching was ordinarily outside of the Mass.

The sixteenth-century Reformers lamented the minimization of preaching in the Sunday Mass, which they believed contributed to the mystification of the Eucharist. Martin Luther's

> pre-eminence in the pulpit derives in part from the earnestness with which he regarded the preaching office. The task of the minister is to expound the Word, in which alone are to be found healing for life's hurts and the balm of eternal blessedness. The preacher must die daily through concern lest he lead his flock astray.[3]

Some Protestant preachers, especially in the earliest days of the Reformation, expended their energies on denouncing various aspects of the established ecclesiastical order, stirring up passions that sometimes led to mobs sacking churches and destroying statues, altars, and other art. However, the major reformers had no intention of inciting riots. They were passionate, of course, in the sense that their revisiting of basic Christian sources had led them to care deeply about what they were discovering, and they were eager and eloquent in sharing what they were finding. In some cases, not surprisingly, congregations subjected to these reforms resented the new preaching, preferring the customs they were used to. Perhaps even more remarkable was that so many were keen to hear more from the reformers, eagerly absorbing the newfound nourishment from the pulpit.

While John Calvin and a few other leaders in the Genevan Reformation were learned people, the first generation of preachers in the city were not, and their preaching reflected it. The situation improved when ministers who were better educated came to Geneva from France, and a strongly text-based preaching began to take hold, supplemented by frequent opportunities for biblical teaching and learning outside of worship.

Preaching in the Genevan tradition followed the pattern of *lectio continua*, i.e., preaching consecutively through a book of the Bible. The Lutheran preachers continued to make use of the lectionaries of the church, but both Reformers, Calvin and Martin Luther, tended to use a verse-by-verse exposition of a specific biblical text in preaching. Luther "took his examples from daily life both in his exposition of the text and his application of the text."[4] He was skillful in the use of down-to-earth images in which his con-

---

3. Bainton, *Here I Stand*, 349.
4. Senn, *Christian Liturgy*, 305.

gregations could recognize their own lives. And yet, there was profundity there as well. After all, Luther had been a professor of Bible at the University of Wittenberg, and he, like other Reformers, knew the biblical languages, Hebrew and Greek. "Year after year Luther preached on the same passages and on the same great events: Advent, Christmas, Epiphany, Lent, Easter, Pentecost. If one now reads through his sermons of thirty years on a single theme, one is amazed at the freshness with which each year he illumined some new aspect."[5]

Gutenberg's relatively new technology, the printing press, had been created in 1440, no doubt strengthening the desirability of literacy by the time of the Reformation, but the oral culture was nevertheless still dominant. The new preaching began to attract those for whom a contemporary proclamation based on Scripture touched people personally as well as intellectually, heart and soul.

John Calvin, who more than any other person shaped the Reformed tradition, had been educated in France as a lawyer, and part of his training involved studying the classical arts of rhetoric represented by Cicero and Quintilian.[6] He used what he had learned both in composing his many writings as well as in his teaching and preaching. For example, the classical rhetoricians taught that it was important to know the capacities of one's audience, and to adjust one's use of language accordingly. That required being able to frame the sermon in the preacher's own words, suitably adapted for those likely to be listening.

Re-Engaging with Sources

But there was more to it than technique. Calvin and Luther were not innovating for the sake of innovation. Their rethinking of the work of the preacher had to do not just with rhetorical strategies, but followed from deep re-engagement with the sources of the Christian faith: the Bible, first and most of all, but also with the doctors of the early church, who had in their own times also been engaged with Scripture and with the struggles of early generations to hear the voice of God in, with, and under the languages of the Bible. It was this encounter with Scripture and early Christian exegesis, thought, practice, and preaching that drove the Reformers to look

---

5. Bainton, *Here I Stand*, 350.
6. Jones, *Calvin and the Rhetoric of Piety*, 13.

critically at everything that Catholic believers and clergy in the sixteenth century had inherited and had learned to take for granted.

Their source-based critique led them to question the Latin Mass. They argued that the church's worship needed to be in the language of the people, as it had been in Rome when Latin was the native language of local Christians. In other words, it needed to be understood spoken in one's own tongue, whether it be Luther's German or Calvin's French or any other. Reformers' fresh encounter with Scripture led them to believe that private Masses were unbiblical. They rejected the common practice of a priest celebrating the Mass daily, alone and without any communicants, sometimes at the same time as other priests at other altars in the same building, using the sacrament as though it should be a more or less private devotion for clerics. And, the Reformers' immersion in basic sources led them to believe that the sacrament without the word preached was neither biblical nor sanctioned by the oldest tradition, and it was risky. When preaching was rare or absent, the sacrament could easily be perceived in a way that cultivated superstition that could obscure or confuse what it meant for it to serve as a means of grace. Preaching often became something like a divine encounter, a sacramental experience that could lead to a deeper perception of the Christ who gives of himself in the sacraments.

In the case of both Martin Luther and John Calvin, the medieval Mass clearly required reform—radical reform for Calvin, more modest for Luther—but both imagined a reformed liturgy that would consist of both the preached word of God and the Eucharist, or Lord's Supper. Luther was more successful than Calvin in achieving a Lord's Day liturgy of word and sacrament every Sunday in his own day, although in generations after Luther, circumstances led to a Lutheran norm in which the sacrament was celebrated only periodically. Calvin achieved even less, being blocked from the beginning by the city Council of Geneva, for whom communing weekly seemed altogether too much of a shock, assuming that such frequency would pose too great a leap for the greater population to understand and accept.

Pre-Reformation Catholics had been accustomed, of course, to a Mass celebrated every Sunday, even though there were rarely communicants. The great majority of the people had acquired such awe of the sacrament that they were reluctant to risk some accidental sacrilege by actually communing. In response, the church had made it a matter of obligation to commune at least once a year, usually on Easter Sunday. Even then, the cup was withheld from the communing laity. The Reformers saw this as a dangerous distortion of the Eucharist. They did not believe that it was biblical to celebrate the sacrament without the participation of all the baptized, so there could be, in their practice, no celebration of the Lord's Supper if there were no communicants other than a priest. The communing assembly was as essential to the sacrament as were bread and wine.

An Engagement with the Holy God

The queasiness of the Geneva Council resulted in a practice neither theologically nor liturgically based. The Council's refusal to permit a weekly Eucharist, a decision based in and for the moment and rooted in their subjective reading of the people's disposition, acquired over time the authority of custom and antiquity. Calvin himself called it a "defect." The unintended result was that preaching became the heart of the service, and for generations, up until today, it has been largely taken for granted that the practice of occasional communion represents some principle derived from the Reformation. Lutheran developments apart from Luther's own practice had similar effects.

The practice of periodic rather than weekly Eucharist has extended beyond those confessional bodies stemming directly from the Reformation, and been imitated by newer churches derived from the older ones. While the Reformers were concerned that the Eucharist without preaching posed a risk, for centuries no one seemed to worry that preaching without the sacrament might pose a risk of its own. When the sacrament is normally absent, for example, it becomes easier for both the people and the preacher to misunderstand what preaching is meant to be. It can be confused with a lecture, or an editorial, or with giving directions. But when the liturgy is organized around both poles rather than only one, word *and* sacrament, it becomes easier to perceive what they both have in common. At its best, each serves, in its own way, as a sacramental act; i.e., a means by which the triune God becomes manifest to the faithful. The purpose and the mission of preaching is just that: to be a sacramental manifestation of the presence of Christ by means of human speech. "The dynamic understanding of the word was at the center of Luther's theology, and also of his understanding of worship and the sacraments. . . . Luther came to appreciate the fact that the word of God is first and foremost God's self-communication, and therefore God's self-disclosure. Therefore the word of God is always an event."[7]

The Reformation accent on the recovery of preaching—and not just any oral presentation, but preaching based on engagement with the biblical text—meant that the Reformers exposed their congregations to a fresh encounter with the very roots of Christian faith. The Reformation itself was enabled by the rejuvenation of classic theology, and one effect was to focus preaching on those things that are both foundational and central to the gospel. Preaching is always *theological*, whether a theology that is intended or one not intended. It is meant to serve an engagement with the holy God, which is what it means to be theo-logical. That does not mean quoting theological textbooks in the sermon. It does mean that a published biblical commentary, while it may help the preacher to focus, ought not get in the way of the preacher's obligation to think through a biblical text theologically, feet on the ground, rather than just citing the thoughts of others in the words of others.

The elevation of the preached word of God juxtaposed to the eucharistic meal whenever it was celebrated did result in significant reforms in practice. Christians communed more frequently than before, even when the sacrament was not celebrated every Sunday. A schedule of quarterly communions in Geneva increased almost everybody's likelihood of communing by a multiple of four every year.

In the medieval church, the sacrament had become more like a spectacle than either a solemn or a joyful occasion. People sometimes ran from parish to parish to try to catch a glimpse of the elevated host the moment the sanctuary bell rang to signal that a transformation had taken place in the very substance of the bread and wine. Post-Reformation, since the active participation of the faithful was considered essential for a true Eucharist, the people were required in the action of the sacrament, participating in the liturgy in their own language and communing in both bread and wine. In both Lutheran and Reformed congregations, the presiding minister preceded the sacrament by offering a scripted admonition beginning with a statement about the meaning of the sacrament, and how to receive it, exhorting the people to prepare themselves in mind and spirit. Luther's included these words:

> I admonish you in Christ that you discern the Testament of Christ in true faith, and, above all, take to heart the words wherein Christ

---
7. Senn, *Christian Liturgy*, 303.

imparts to us his body and his blood for the remission of our sins. That you remember and give thanks for his boundless love which he proved to us when he redeemed us from God's wrath, sin, death, and hell by his own blood. And that in this faith you externally receive the bread and the wine, i.e. his body and his blood, as the pledge and guarantee of this.[8]

Calvin's admonition followed the words of institution, that were read as a kind of warrant before beginning the eucharistic prayer. (He was concerned that, if used within the prayer, it might imply that the words themselves effected a consecration, as had been the teaching of the pre-Reformation church.) Calvin's admonition was much longer than Luther's. Along with a reminder that all feel "much frailty and misery from not having perfect faith, but being inclined to unbelief and distrust," he said, "Let us therefore understand that this sacrament is a medicine for the spiritually poor and sick, and that the only worthiness which our Savior requires in us is to know ourselves, so as to be dissatisfied with our vices, and have all our pleasure, joy and contentment in him alone."[9]

In both the Lutheran and Reformed liturgies, the biblical story of the Last Supper was highlighted by the prominent use of Jesus' words in the thanksgiving prayer itself (Luther) or preceding it (Calvin), spoken in the local language in both cases, so that the people might actually understand the words and be edified. The importance of the words of institution remained, even though the purpose of their use was understood differently than before the Reformation.

Preparing for Heaven

However valuable the Protestant reforms may have been, it is nevertheless true that it was the Roman Church that defined the issues that framed the subsequent debates about the holy meal, and the Catholic position became less flexible after the Reformation than before it. Sacramental theology is never a peripheral matter because it is directly linked to basic doctrine in every confessional community, Roman Catholic or Protestant. The medieval church thought of the Eucharist in terms of its efficacy: what happened in the sacramental actions and what were its benefits. The Reformers, critiquing the Roman Church's teaching in such matters, nevertheless took up

---

8. Jasper and Cuming, *Prayers of the Eucharist*, 197.
9. Jasper and Cuming, *Prayers of the Eucharist*, 217.

the conversation without contesting the point at which the debate had begun. The Roman Church insisted that the bread and wine truly "becomes" the body and blood of Christ, even though such transformation was not visibly or physically discernable, implying, in effect, that the sacramental elements were equivalent in some sense to an extension of the incarnation. The Mass was a kind of sacrifice, lifting up Christ's death on the cross as an offering to God in exchange for the forgiveness of the sins of the baptized, thus clearing the way for the faithful to be welcomed in heaven after death. The English translation of the Roman Canon (eucharistic prayer) included this petition:

> Humbly we implore you, almighty God, bid these offerings be carried by the hands of your holy angel to your altar on high, before your divine majesty, so that those of us who by sharing in the sacrifice at this altar shall receive the body and blood of your Son, may be filled with every grace and heavenly blessing.[10]

The Reformers, particularly Luther, utterly rejected the notion of a sacrifice being made in the sacrament itself. There could be no repetition, or even suggestion of a repetition, of Christ's sacrifice on the cross. (It should be noted that contemporary Roman Catholic theology is more nuanced when it comes to understanding "sacrifice" than it appeared to the Reformers in the sixteenth century.)

The Romans had declared that the fundamental issue was the real presence of Christ in the sacrament as represented by the doctrine of transubstantiation. Disputing the doctrine, the Reformers conceded, in various ways, that the Romans were right to speak of real presence, but considered the established church to be mistaken in concluding that transubstantiation accurately described that presence. Luther offered another way of understanding real presence; Zwingli, the reformer of Zurich, said that Luther had it wrong—the meal was basically a kind of memorial. Calvin agreed with Zwingli that Luther didn't have it right and with Luther that Zwingli didn't have it right, and Calvin offered his own view that, incidentally, seems to resemble something more nearly like the position of the Eastern churches. Thus proceeded the debate, which has not been resolved even today.

The debates about real presence in a time of reform proceeded as they did because both sides worked from similar presumptions: the Eucharist

---

10. Mazza, *Eucharistic Prayers*, 52.

was part of the whole picture of nourishing the people of God, preparing them for their own journeys to heaven. As early as the era in which the New Testament writings were being composed, some Christians were already becoming anxious that the promised kingdom of God was slower to come than they had expected. The first Christian believers anticipated that the *parousia*, Christ's return to inaugurate his eschatological reign, would come soon—even during their lifetimes. When some believers died and the *parousia* had not yet come, they required reassurance.

> But we do not want you to be uninformed, brothers and sisters, about those who have died, so that you may not grieve as others do who have no hope.... God will bring with him those who have died ... so that whether we are awake or asleep we may live with him. (1 Thess 4:13—5:11)

As generations came and went, it must have felt necessary to adjust to a different way of thinking about how, in between Christ's resurrection and his "second coming," God is at work for our redemption. The church began to frame God's work of salvation in such a way as to highlight the existential concerns of individual believers. Attention became more narrowly directed toward "heaven." Christians, like all other mortals, were frequently reminded of their own mortality. With the apparent delay of the *basileia* and its renewal of all things appearing ever more distant, it must have seemed more pastorally urgent to address the ever-threatening crisis of death. The end of life, of course, was all too familiar in the days when life expectancy was far shorter than we are accustomed to. So quietly as to be unremarkable, the eschatological vision of Scripture and the early church became marginalized in Christian piety and teaching.

Quite probably the themes of "going to heaven" and *basileia*, the reign of God realized on earth, had coexisted in some sense and overlapped from the beginning. But, as the future reign of God became marginalized in ordinary piety, even though not denied, the ultimate redemption was nevertheless abstracted into irrelevance. One should not be surprised that with the passage of time, the eschatological hope began to be upstaged by the more immediate promise of going to heaven (perhaps by way of purgatory), surely more personally urgent, and certainly not as likely to be postponed as long as the new heaven and new earth had been. When persecution and martyrdom were a shared communal memory kept alive by the cult of the saints, the anticipation of heaven's refuge must have pushed to one side the hope of a cosmic redemption. Under the circumstances, it was even tempting to conclude that maybe the "kingdom of God" referred to the church itself, a "kingdom" that was in competition with various earthly kingdoms. In fact, according to Jürgen Moltmann, faith in the coming *basileia* did not so much fade away as it was "transformed into a political and ecclesiastical self-confidence" with the church itself "claiming to be the earthly heir to Christ's authority."[11]

The Reformers Accepted the Terms of the Discussion Set by Rome

Of course, the ancient Greek philosophers retained some influence for generations, particularly among the well educated. Certainly Thomas Aquinas, as late as the thirteenth century, made use of Aristotelian thought as he developed his view of transubstantiation. And Plato had conceived of the human being as both a body and a soul, the soul leaving the body at death, surviving without it. This view is certainly not that of the Bible, but it continues to be a conventional view among Christians even today, and serves in its own way to focus attention on "saving one's soul," the personal journey after death.

When the ultimate Christian hope began to be focused on "going to heaven," it is not surprising that the focus of ministry should have turned to providing counsel and practical means to anxious and hopeful individuals to lead them to make use of the disciplines and resources of the church. Since the concern about one's own salvation can be so basic, and since it calls for consistent pastoral guidance and support, once it becomes conceived in such individualized terms, it subtly shifts the center of theological gravity. Inevitably, the accent on how the sacraments were to be understood evolved accordingly when the hope of heaven took central place, at the expense of the hope of Christ's ultimate reign. Baptism, Eucharist, and certainly preaching needed to be understood in a way that served the immediate challenge: to prepare people for eternity.

By the sixteenth century, the gospel message had, for practical purposes, long before shifted to focus on personal salvation, achieved one by one. The shift was gradual enough, and had been so little noticed, that Reformers did not question it. Rather, the question that took all their attention was about *how* one gets to heaven. Both Catholics and Protestants

---

11. Green, *Imagining Theology*, 183. The first quote is from Moltmann, the second by Green interpreting Moltmann.

shared the same grounds as their opponents when they debated teaching and practices that had become increasingly unquestionable in the Roman Church. Both the very specific rule-based authority of the Roman Church to lay out the terms of salvation, and the grace-based testimony of the Protestants were, each in its own way, oriented to individual souls. The debate became about whether people are saved by "works"—things they need to do, including making use of aids and obligations provided by the church and only by the church—or by grace alone, through faith.

It seems that everyone on both the establishment and the reforming sides more or less agreed that the efficacy of the sacraments (and, for the Reformers, also the efficacy of preaching) was to guide and support the faithful into heaven, which happens one by one. The major issues in dispute in the Reformation and Counter-Reformation focused on issues of salvation to which the Bible is certainly not indifferent, while paying little or no attention to the Bible's framing of ultimate questions about redemption on a much larger screen. If the big screen picture had become lost in sacramental theology, it had equally become lost in preaching. This is our legacy whether we are Catholic or Protestant. N. T. Wright notes that "the Reformers failed to challenge the larger heaven-and-hell framework itself (which Eastern theologians challenge to this day) or to think through what new creation and resurrection would actually mean or how they might come about. . . . That vision of a nonbodily ultimate 'heaven' is a direct legacy of Plato."[12]

The Christian Hope Narrowed

Of course, American Christians will be aware of their history of periodic great awakenings, the predecessors of the nineteenth-century revival meetings extending well into the twentieth. The revival meeting was about making conversions, and the conversions were about setting your trajectory toward heaven rather than hell. Many twenty-first century churches were shaped historically by the revival model, so that the purpose of every service is meant to make conversions, and the mission of preaching is to lead each one to make a decision for Christ, essential for those bound for heaven.

Whatever values one may find in this effort to draw people to the gospel, it shares with the medieval church and the churches of the Reformation

12. Wright, *Day the Revolution Began*, 33–34.

an unintentionally narrow view of the Christian hope, reduced to the issue of one's own personal destiny. For those churches that preach a very literal return of Christ, the *parousia* is understood as a sorting and separating event that is, once again, about each person's own ultimate future. While this is understandable in terms of our personal, existential interests, it quietly lays aside the eschatological images projected over and over in Christ's boundary-crossing ministry.

In recent biblical study and liturgical theology, we are experiencing a new interest in the eschatological picture, though not in the way it has been imagined by those for whom it is chiefly about separating people. The renewed eschatological interest is evident when we turn to the sacrament as manifestation of the *basileia*, the reign of God. Sacramental theology, and the Eucharist in particular, shifts the scale of redemption from one-by-one to the cosmos itself, and all who are in it. In the heavenly banquet images in Scripture we are led to a big-picture redemption, a cosmic resurrection, a transfiguration of heaven and earth, where God's expansive generosity is clearly visible in the reign of Christ, whose embrace reaches beyond conventionally pious judgments. Sacramental theology rightfully and inevitably leads us to recognize the sacramental mission of preaching as well. When preaching and the Eucharist are normally experienced side-by-side, the preacher is more likely to recognize how it is possible even for preaching itself to become food and drink, nourishing us in anticipation of the messianic banquet.

A Preacher's Reflections: Endings

Reading the obituaries in the twenty-first century, one might notice that almost no one dies. Instead, they "pass away." Or, even more awkwardly, they "pass." No indication of where they might be passing to, just "passed." The choice of language is no doubt intended to soften the hard words, helping to keep actual dying at arm's length. "Passing" language might have fit in the case of the family member who died just short of his 102nd birthday. He died quickly and quietly not long after enjoying a good breakfast, more than a century after he was born. But I think it doesn't work as well for, say, people like a young mother in Idaho, accidentally shot and killed a few years ago by her two-year old while she was shopping at Walmart. In that case, "passed" is just too gentle. It doesn't do it. And I suspect it wouldn't do, either, for the only son of the widow in Nain, who could no doubt have been expected to live quite a bit longer than he did (Luke 7:11–17).

As best I can understand the Bible, death is always a crisis. Not necessarily a tragedy, but always a crisis, even when it is welcome; even when it's a relief. It may not seem like a crisis when someone dies quietly, full of years. But even in that case, it is a crisis for the one who has died. It is a crisis in a couple of ways. For one thing it is, of course, a moment of ending—a real ending. Whatever is undone is left undone, and will be always. And even when there seems to be nothing left unfinished, nothing that still needs to be repaired, death is still a crisis.

Maybe just because crises upset us, we feel inclined to pretend that they are not crises. Somewhere—probably from the Greeks—Christians picked up the idea that a person is made up of detachable parts. At the moment of death, the body dies, but the spirit lives on, simply flying away. If that should be the case, then maybe death is not a crisis—or, at least not such a big deal for the one whose soul has been liberated from the body. But it is another thing, isn't it, if death claims the whole person, body and soul?

In Jesus' time, there was a division among Jewish believers about what happens to one who has died. The Sadducees were the more orthodox party, believing that life simply ended. The Pharisees, who are the forebears of modern Judaism, represented a view that had gained adherents in the period between the Old and New Testaments. The Pharisees believed that, in the final consummation, there would be a general resurrection. The Christian view is maybe a little of both, but not quite the same as either one. Christian faith takes its cue specifically from the resurrection of the Lord. Human beings are not partly mortal and partly immortal, as though after dying the soul simply sheds the no-longer-needed burden of the body. No. Resurrection implies something quite different. The dead are just dead unless and until God acts. The dead are clearly, unequivocally, dead; utterly dependent on God to effect any change in status. So, the appropriate word is "crisis."

As for the survivors, though, "crisis" isn't always the best word—not in every case. It is hardly a shock when someone 102 years old dies, and the tears shed are not likely to be bitter tears. But there are tears, of course, and tears are entirely appropriate. Sometimes well-meaning folks try to talk each other out of their tears, but surely they are misguided. Those who are left behind are not immune to the enormous significance of endings, no matter how well they may have braced themselves to face it.

I wonder about the widow in the village of Nain, accompanying her son to the cemetery. We know absolutely nothing personal about her, of course, but maybe it's fair to speculate a little. In those days, life was more often short, and old age was rare. We don't know the age of the son, but Jesus called him, "young man" (Luke 7:14). His widowed mother was more likely in her thirties or her forties than in her sixties or seventies. Without a male relative to lean on, she would have been extremely vulnerable. It may be that her pure sorrow, her deep sadness, might have overwhelmed any concerns about her own welfare, but she would not have been entirely out of line were she to have felt angry and distraught at the circumstances, finding herself so bereft, so helpless.

Jesus and his disciples and others who were following them walked into the village of Nain, and found that they had stumbled into a funeral procession. Jesus assessed the situation, identified the chief mourner, and "he had compassion for her" (7:13). Luke tells us that he spoke to her. He said, "Do not weep." John Carroll thinks the Greek is better translated, "Don't go on weeping."[13] Is Jesus scolding her for her tears, do you think? Encouraging her to keep a stiff upper lip? To think positively? To look on the bright side? To count her blessings? Or is he, like so many others, hoping that she would just put her grief away for a while to spare others from being exposed to it?

I don't think his words should be heard in any of those ways. He was not setting expectations for a certain kind of restrained behavior. I think he was speaking as a parent might to a child who wakens in the night, disturbed by a bad dream. His tone and demeanor would speak louder than the actual words. "Don't cry" or "Don't go on crying" just means, "I'm here. I love you. It will be okay."

Then Jesus stepped forward, stopped the pallbearers, and addressed the corpse: "Young man, I say to you, rise!" (7:14). Bystanders must have wondered whether Jesus had lost his mind. The dead, after all, neither see nor hear. But, Luke tells us, "The dead man sat up and began to speak" (7:15).

A Glimpse of the Basileia

Is it wise to doubt that the Holy God has the power to repair the world? To set it right? The power to overcome the power of death to cancel us out

---

13. Carroll, *Luke: A Commentary*, 166.

and plunge us into an eternal silence? Or even to fashion a new creation? The whole point of the Gospel writers is to testify to their conviction that wherever Jesus was, God's strength, God's determination, God's power to make a new creation made itself felt and tasted and seen. God's reign, God's dominion, God's kingdom, was at work in and through Jesus, wherever he went. In the new creation, all tears will be wiped away, and all manner of brokenness repaired. For now, we have only glimpses of that new creation, but it was made manifest on that day in Nain. Of the young man, we know nothing. We know nothing of his character, nothing of his faith, nothing of the circumstances of his death. There is no sign that he was supernaturally interviewed or vetted to see if he met the criteria for divine mercy. All we know is that he was a young, dead man, with a weeping mother. He who could not possibly hear anything heard Jesus' voice calling to him, and he sat up. And who wouldn't?

The young man's death and his mother's grief both matter, of course. But while Jesus' action is about him, it is also not exclusively about him. The young man's awakening from death, to live perhaps a full and maybe even long life, serves not as the end of all dying, but as a promise of and anticipation of the *basileia*, a transfigured creation, in which all things will be made new, and death will be no more. Jesus himself is the guarantor of that promise, and the agent by which it shall be made manifest.

4

Preaching the Cosmic Scope of God's Redemption

A Knock at the Door

A FACEBOOK FRIEND POSTED a note describing his experience when two women came to the door of his home representing an evangelical congregation a few miles away. They invited him and his family to visit their church.

> I thanked them and said I was an [officer] at First . . . Church downtown, thinking that would quickly be the end of their visit. But instead, they continued to give us reasons why we should attend their church, and talked about how wonderful the pastor was. . . . They asked me to "take a look at the information in the card, to make sure I'm going to heaven . . ." In the card, there was a picture of the pastor . . . and underneath the picture, the first thing it said was, "Everyone is a sinner," and later, "not everybody is going to heaven."

My friend wrote, "This is not evangelism, it's low-level sales . . . it totally misses the point of being a Christ-follower. This is the gospel of fear and manipulation, meant to frighten people, and it's toxic."[1] This experience, not unusual, is an example of the risk of distorting Christian faith when it is narrowed down to who is "going to heaven," and, especially, when it claims to know who is not.

1. Facebook post and personal communication with Andrew Perkins, April 15, 2021, are used by permission.

The ecumenical efforts to recover the eschatological focus of our faith leads us in a very different direction than the preaching of the second coming that has become traditional in those Christian circles whose focus is on the risk of being personally excluded from heaven. It is, in fact, a crude exclusiveness that has contributed hugely to mainstream churches' aversion to eschatology, the "big picture" of our redemption. Where exclusion has been the dominant understanding of the reign of God, with grace reserved for a few who have managed to qualify for it, the *parousia* (Christ's messianic return in glory) has been interpreted as a moment for division: the righteous from the unrighteous, the faithful from the faithless, the older son from the prodigal, those who follow the rules from those who don't, and the "rules" are never to be changed because they were laid down a long time ago and it is possible to cite the chapter and verse to prove it. Since judgment is taken to imply the ultimate separation of the "godly" from the "ungodly," it invites division here and now. Some are "in," some are "out," and no reconciliation or even much give and take are possible between the two perspectives, one individualistic, the other cosmic.

A Preacher's Reflections: The Spirit Still Has Something to Say

In Jesus' so-called "farewell discourse," he did not draw such dramatic lines, as though everything that God might say or do had already been said and done. John's gospel lets us listen in as Jesus offered something like "last words" to his disciples before his final crisis. Nevertheless, there's a lot left unsaid, apparently. Because Jesus cautions the disciples, "I still have many things to say to you, but you cannot bear them now" (John 16:12).

A program on NPR featured reactions of people who had once been told by some authoritative adult, "You'll understand when you're older." That kind of attempted trump card, meant to put you in your (immature) place, is not usually received well. Who knows how the disciples took it, but Jesus told them that there were some things he just could not explain to them at the moment. "You cannot bear them now."

One wonders what he might have had in mind. Probably he was thinking of the near future. Maybe thinking that, at his moment of crisis, his disciples would desert him. TMI, Too Much Information to manage beforehand. Or maybe he could have been imagining the trials and joys they would experience when they gathered the courage to proclaim his resurrection. But surely they weren't ready for that, either. Or, maybe he was pondering how, before many years, the Romans would sack Jerusalem and destroy the temple, and the new center of the Jesus movement would shift from Jewish to gentile territory: Rome, Alexandria. Unimaginable!

Or—and this is pure speculation—his words could apply equally well to things that would happen in the far distant future—things they could not begin to wrap their minds around. Because in every generation we face new situations, new discoveries, new experiences that we have to come to terms with some way, somehow. It would be nice for us, living in times of bewildering conflict, if Jesus had offered some explicit instruction that would answer all our twenty-first-century questions. Maybe if he had spelled out what to do about exponential population growth, or reflected on the downside of burning fossil fuels and pumping carbon dioxide into the air. Crucial issues are these, but no way visible on their radar screen in the first century. Maybe he could have said something helpful about gender confusion; or clarified who should be in charge of making decisions about reproduction; or just calmed down the folks who were bound to be all worked up over issues of marriage equality. But to anticipate twenty-first-century issues (and all the others in-between) would have left those first-century disciples utterly confused.

In one congregation a young woman was distributing Bibles to third-graders. She told them it was the "answer book." One or two in the congregation cringed. Yes, of course, the Bible has some answers. But the Bible is not like one's old algebra book, where the answers to all the questions were printed in the back. One reason for that is that the Bible wasn't written to answer questions that haven't been asked yet, or are just being asked now for the first time. "I have many things to say to you, but you cannot bear them now."

So, then, does that mean that God has already said everything that's going to be said, and has nothing at all to add as new situations present themselves? Are we really left completely on our own then? I don't think that is the case. Jesus promised the disciples, "When the Spirit of truth comes, he will guide you into all the truth" (John 16:13). The Holy Spirit, then, is going to work with us as new occasions arise, teaching new duties. But how? How does the Holy Spirit work with us?

Preaching the Cosmic Scope of God's Redemption

How Does the Holy Spirit Reveal New Things?

Well, the Mormons believed that the Creator told Joseph Smith that he needed to marry more women in addition to the wife he already had. Neither their ages nor whether they were already married mattered; and, Smith contended that God had also told him not to allow any people of African ancestry into his new priesthood. In other words, the Holy One supposedly provided direct, unambiguous directions. Of course later, God supposedly had a change of mind, and directly mandated the about-face to Smith's successors.

Similarly, in 1870 the first Vatican Council decided that the pope, when he speaks officially in his capacity as Vicar of Christ on earth, can deliver a direct revelation that the faithful must receive as infallible.

Receiving a direct revelation like a news bulletin from on high would be helpful, wouldn't it? Such a thing might solve some difficult dilemmas! But I don't for a minute believe that it works that way. The Holy Spirit is more likely to speak to the church organically. In other words, not necessarily from the top down, but often percolating from the bottom up. Or, even speaking to the church sideways, so to speak, in voices from outside the church. The Holy Spirit speaks, not usually directly or unambiguously, but often so quietly as to risk being unrecognized. Hesitantly, the church begins to hear what the Spirit is saying, supported by its prayer, discernment, debate, conflict that both confuses and clarifies, and very often accompanied by the kind of anxiety and disruption that precedes a new consensus.

The Holy Spirit speaks to the church, and we find ourselves rejecting customs highly valued for centuries. The divine right of kings, trashed. Slavery, discarded, and race-based privilege no longer credible. Male domination, rejected. Caste systems, overruled. Barefoot and pregnant, so over. Disdain for those who don't fit the prevailing patterns of masculinity or femininity, getting over it. The Holy Spirit speaks, pushing against our resistance, shaking us up, and, at last, leading us to consent to what's new to us, but not new to God.

Of course, we have to be careful here. It's easy to be misled. So in his first letter, John counsels: "Beloved, do not believe every spirit, but test the spirits to see whether they are from God" (1 John 4:1). Not every new idea or novel proposal is good. It is not hard to find new trends that are basically obnoxious, and worse, actually spiritual poison. So, how can we "test the spirits"? How do we recognize the Holy Spirit's work, and turn a deaf ear to malignant or trivial spirits?

Jesus told the disciples, "When the Spirit comes, he will guide you into all the truth . . . he will take what is mine and declare it to you" (John 16:12a–14). In other words, the Spirit is always unfolding more of what we have already seen in Jesus Christ: the Spirit will "take what is mine and declare it to you." A lot of what we know about Jesus is derived from what he did and who he was, not depending on his words alone. Jesus Christ, the boundary breaker. Jesus Christ, tablemate of sinners; the one who stood up in the synagogue at Nazareth to point out how the God of Israel had sometimes favored strangers of other tribes and other religions over them, the chosen (Luke 4:24–28). Jesus Christ, who drew outcasts to himself, who healed the broken in spirit, body, or mind. Jesus Christ, who embraced those whom culture and religion shunned as sources of contamination. In him, God reveals God's own character and disposition towards us. "All that the Father has is mine," Jesus said (John 16:15).

Healing the Whole Creation

If I understand it at all, the gospel of Jesus Christ is the good news that God is going to heal the whole creation. In the biblical stories of the lame made straight and strong, the blind given sight, the deaf recovering their hearing, the speechless given a voice, those eaten up by disease becoming whole again, sinners being forgiven and the dead being raised, God is offering us a preview of how things are going to turn out. The New Testament healings aren't just sympathetic stories about a handful of people far away and long ago. They represent a kind of down payment on the future. They represent a graphic promise, rooted in the faithfulness, the reliability of the God who makes the promise. The disorder of the present, the uncertainty of the moment, the bad news that nips at our heels tells the sad truth about how things are, but it is not the whole truth. This is good news, isn't it?

Aren't we all just holding our breath for some good news? Good advice has its place, but it's not the same as good news. And in these days of crisis, it would seem as though the good news we are waiting for needs to be even bigger than the good news of an engagement, a new baby, an unprecedented rise in the stock market, or that someone has made an offer on the house.

But there is more good news. God invites us to play at least a small part in shaping that new creation that's been solemnly promised in the blessed resurrection of the Lord. Now and then, here and there, with God's help, our own touch becomes a healing touch. Our mortal words may calm a storm. The gift of our presence, turning *toward* the hurting folks instead of *away* from them—now and then, the gift of ourselves pushes back the chaos, scatters the demons, makes a peaceful space where folks can begin to get in touch with their "right minds." Not because you or I, or the whole of Christ's church, are either wise or strong, but because God is wise, and strong. Not because we are promise keepers, but because God is a promise keeper. What we see in Jesus is what God is preparing for us: a new creation, a redeemed creation, a demon-free creation, a transfigured creation, the dazzlingly bright day that follows the days of storms.

Jesus said, "[The Holy Spirit] will take what is mine and declare it to you." What the Holy Spirit does, I think, is less like sending out a news bulletin and more like giving us a heart transplant. Fleming Rutledge, the Episcopal preacher, has written that "It takes effort to care when one is not directly involved."[2] Indeed. Rutledge quotes Luis Segundo, a Jesuit from Uruguay. He notes that "the world that is satisfying to us [the affluent] is utterly devastating to [the poor and powerless]." For those of us who are financially secure, who have support systems in place, who know where to go for help when we have a problem, we really have to make an effort to understand people who have none of those things. We're tempted to judge them as though they are propped up by all the same supports that are propping us up. But for them, the same world is experienced as "utterly devastating." It might make us feel less vulnerable if we let ourselves presume that anybody who really tries can stand on their own two feet. It's at this point that we need the heart transplant. The Holy Spirit can strengthen us so that we learn to care even when our own lives are not at stake.

Can You Hear Me Now?

Whatever the Holy Spirit has to reveal to us will always be entirely consistent with the character of the God already made known in Christ. But we must listen carefully, and listen together. The Holy Spirit is still speaking to the church. Typically, only a few hear the Spirit's voice at first. Somebody takes notice of an injustice, and calls attention to it, but few others pay attention. Then, other voices join in, and the volume rises, and some minds begin to change, and then comes the pushback. There are outcries, there is anguish, there are counterarguments, but when the Spirit is speaking, sooner or later

2. Rutledge, *Crucifixion*, 122.

the greater number start to see injustice where they used to see a comfortable status quo. And when a tipping point is reached, the whole church, even whole societies, experience a change of mind. Sometimes the Spirit speaks through Christians first; sometimes the church follows where others lead. But the Spirit cannot be locked up or locked out.

A heart transplant. So, things that aren't issues for me or my family, but may be issues for you and yours, matter to both of us. The holy God who is above and beyond us has come to stand beside us in the person of Jesus Christ. The self-same God who is both above us and standing beside us is also at work within us and among us, before us and behind us in the mystery of the Holy Spirit, exchanging warm hearts to replace hard hearts. What we have conceived narrowly, the Holy Spirit enables us to see expansively, with a grace wider than our conventional boundary making. The Spirit, Jesus says, "will take what is mine and declare it to you."

The history of the church includes the Crusades and an inquisition, and no doubt many other unremarked but painful instances of Christians defining as hopeless all sorts of people, good as well as bad, who were apparently on what had been perceived to be the *wrong* team. *Kyrie eleison! Christ, have mercy!* But the Holy Spirit still nudges us, troubles us, leads us to see what was there for us to see all along if we had not been so afraid to open our eyes. "But a second time the voice answered from heaven, 'What God has made clean, you must not call profane'" (Acts 10:9). These words addressed from heaven to the apostle Peter may well apply in a larger context than even he had perceived. Come, Holy Spirit!

A Preacher's Reflections: The Basileia and the Healing Judge

The eschatological vision, then, is not to be taken as a threat, implying that those who are different from us, or disagree with us, or don't "know" what we believe we "know" are to be discounted, written off, dismissed—"not going to heaven."

The Bible points to "the day of the Lord," or "the kingdom of God." We speak of the reign of God, or the "second coming." The Bible reminds us that the *parousia*, which introduces Christ's glorious reign, is also a day of judgment. But even so, the news is good. "Then shall all the trees of the forest sing for joy before the Lord, for he comes to judge the earth. O give thanks to the Lord, for he is good" (1 Chr 16:33–34). When we hear the word "judgment" we tend to cringe. And well we ought to if it should be human judgments we are cringing from. Human beings tend to get their judgments wrong. Human judgments are often way over the top, out of proportion, off base, even cruel. But this is no judgment administered by mortals, with all our hidden agendas and notorious fallibility. We're talking about divine judgment, and divine judgment is not based on biased or partial information.

Divine judgment is not subject to bribes, or payoffs, or favors exchanged. Divine judgment is not fueled by rage built up over a lifetime—rage misdirected towards any available target. Divine judgment comes to the *rescue*. That's why even the natural world rejoices, why even "the trees of the forest sing for joy"—because God's judgment is the only thing strong enough, big enough, fair enough, to meet the distortions, the unfairness, the utter foolishness, great and small, whether among the nations or among the members of a household. Divine judgment is the only answer to a world that's clearly bent out of shape, out of balance, tilted in favor of winners determined to take all, all, all. Divine judgment is the only saving help when human systems can no more than approximate justice. It's the only remedy when even our best efforts fall short.

God's project is cosmic redemption—the repair of the whole creation. The apostle Paul wrote that God "has made known to us the mystery of his will, according to his good pleasure that he set forth in Christ, as a plan for the fullness of time, to gather up all things in him, things in heaven and things on earth" (Eph 1:9-10). It's about you and me, sure enough—but not just about you and me. It's about a new heaven and a new earth.

Of course, as wonderful as a dramatic new creation must be, even ordinary changes have the power to unsettle us. Students of psychology remind us that it is not just sickness or grieving or unemployment or a financial crisis that causes stress. Stress also accompanies happy things: falling in love, getting married, buying a house, retirement, winning the lottery. When Jesus warns his disciples that they may experience the coming of God's ultimate reign as a jolt, as a shock to the system, as a sense that the whole world is melting away and the very landscape is in a state of upheaval, he is telling the truth. A cosmic redemption is cause for rejoicing—but it promises to shake everything to the foundations. It's good news, but it will feel like a crisis, like a winnowing, a sorting out. Jesus uses a heart-stopping image to heighten the sense that something crucial is at stake. In Noah's time, he said,

> they were eating and drinking, marrying and giving in marriage, until the day Noah entered the ark, and they knew nothing until the flood came and swept them all away, so too will be the coming of the Son of Man. (Matt 24:38–39)

Jesus used such an alarming image to warn his disciples against complacency and indifference. He offers an example of complacency. The Noah story paints a picture of ordinary times, when people were going about their daily business, shopping for groceries, preparing meals, enjoying a little drink, getting married, dancing at a daughter's wedding. "And they knew nothing until the flood came and swept them all away." Like those folks in Noah's time, most of us spend our lives focusing on what's immediately at hand. We start most days with a list, either written down or in our heads: Take your violin to school. Sign the report card. Stop at the ATM. Lunch with a client. Update Facebook page. Soccer practice. Pick up dry cleaning. Revise the Christmas card list. Our to-do lists are different, but not too different. They have in common that they divert our attention from the bigger picture, from the panoramic view of the times and circumstances that form the context for our lives.

Where Is It All Headed?

A church offered several vocational groups: separate discussion groups for nurses, teachers, doctors, lawyers, etc. Each group shared case studies from their own daily work. In the lawyers' group, after much job talk, the moderator felt led to ask: "Do lawyers ever talk about justice?" The silence was profound and sustained. Similarly, groups of pastors may be heard comparing stories about church finances, membership statistics, denominational quarrels, stories sad or hilarious from parish life—but rarely about salvation, about judgment, about grace, about ultimate things.

The newspaper carried a story about US soldiers who had arrived at their posting in the far reaches of Afghanistan. As they scanned the bleak landscape, one voiced the question in everyone's mind: "What are we doing here?" That's the right kind of question, whether in Afghanistan, or at church, or in your workplace or high on a builder's scaffold, or at school, or sitting in the box seats or the cheap seats at the game, or in Congress. What are we doing here? We've all got our heads down. Our eyes are focused only a few steps ahead. We choose not to think about the bigger question: What are we doing here? And, the related one: Where are we headed?

And it's at exactly this point that the Christian gospel departs from the atheist or agnostic point of view. The logical conclusion of the atheist or the agnostic is that our collective human life is headed, ultimately, nowhere—nowhere at all—so there's no point in even asking the question. But the Christian gospel takes its cue from the resurrection of the Lord. We take the resurrection of the Lord as God's solemn promise that we are headed somewhere. And Christ will be in it, and there will be some kind of judgment in it, because without a God who's big enough to sort it all out, there just plain won't be any salvation at all. This may seem strange to those for whom it seems as though everything is going just fine, thank you, and all it would take is a little tweak here and there to clean everything up and make it become everything it ought to be. But our situation is not one that can be cured with a tweak. We require a redemption that is cosmic in scope; that is, one that includes even those we might choose not to include.

Through the prophet Malachi, God promises to send a messenger. "Indeed, he is coming, says the LORD of hosts. But who can endure the day of his coming, and who can stand when he appears? For he is like a refiner's fire and like fuller's soap" (Mal 3:1b–2a). The old creation will be shaken, the old heaven and the old earth will be turned upside down. Everything ugly and cruel and wrong and unfair, whether the loss of a child or a holocaust; whether injustice at the hands of a rapacious corporation or at the hands of corrupt public officials—everything will be subjected to the refiner's fire, the fuller's soap. Neither intended to destroy, but to clean up. It will be judgment, for love's sake. It will burn and it will sting, for love's sake. Judgment, for the sake of a new beginning. Judgment, because God is good, and God is immensely generous, and God will not abandon you or me or all the nations—will not leave us alone in our sins and self-deception. Judgment is grace, judgment is kindness, judgment is good news. Judgment is the utterly necessary and welcome threshold that leads to a new heaven and a new earth. Hold in mind the panoramic view. "Keep awake . . . for you do not know on what day your Lord is coming" (Matt 24:42).

The Bigger Question

Imagining that the question should be "Who is going to heaven?" or "Who *isn't* going to heaven?" is too small, too narrow. The Jesus Christ we see in our Bible is one who, in his own ministry, crossed and even broke boundaries. He healed on the Sabbath although it was technically against the Torah.

Sometimes, compassion requires breaking the rule (John 5:1–18). And Jesus accepted the plea of the Syro-Phoenician woman, whose earnestness impressed him even as she took the risk of trying to show him a breadth and expanse to his ministry that had not been evident to him (Mark 7:24–30; Matt 15:21–28). He had a conversation with the Samaritan woman, even though it crossed boundaries honorable people were supposed to take seriously (John 4:1–42). In other words, although he had been schooled in the rules of Torah and those of decency and custom, and respected them, he ventured, nevertheless, to where he was needed, even though to go there invited scorn and rejection. And he is needed, too, in the cross-shaped places. Those who are cursed in the eyes of God need him, too. God's ultimate redemptive purpose is not likely to be sabotaged by the fact that hell is host not just to the innocent who may have fallen into it by accident, but also to those who may well have earned their ticket there. David Bentley Hart, an Eastern Orthodox scholar of religion and a philosopher, writes that

> Jesus speaks of a final judgment, and uses many metaphors to describe the unhappy lot of the condemned. Many of these are metaphors of destruction, like the annihilation of chaff or brambles in ovens, or the final death of body and soul in the Valley of Hinnom (Gehenna). Others are metaphors of exclusion, like the sealed doors of wedding feasts. A few, a very few, are images of imprisonment and torture; but even then, in the relevant verses, those punishments are depicted as having only a limited term (Matthew 5:26; 18:34; Luke 12:47-48; 59). Nowhere is there any description of perpetual cruelty presided over by Satan. . . . On the other hand, however, there are a remarkable number of passages in the New Testament, several of them from Paul's writings, that appear instead to promise a final salvation of all persons and all things, and in the most unqualified terms.[3]

Once again, "What we have conceived narrowly, the Holy Spirit enables us to see expansively, with a grace wider than our conventional boundary making."

---

3. Hart, *That All Shall Be Saved*, 93–94.

5

Preaching and Its Trinitarian Foundation

The grace of the Lord Jesus Christ, the love of God, and the communion of the Holy Spirit . . .
(2 Cor 13:13)

A Preacher's Reflections

THE CHRISTIAN FAITH IS, at its very center, Trinitarian. That is, in fact, the way our faith is shaped. Not surprising, then, that eucharistic prayers in our various service books are Trinitarian in both structure and content.

If you have visited the famous Dome of the Rock in Jerusalem, your guide may have pointed out the Arabic inscription around the interior of the dome. It is from Sura 19 in the Qur'an: "God could not take to himself any son." It was inscribed in that highly visible place intentionally to scorn the doctrine of the Trinity, and specifically to rebuke the Christians.

One can sympathize with the Muslims, don't you think? How can one be three? Or three be one? But we are not really talking about simple arithmetic here. We speak of one and three of necessity, because we lack the ability to conceptualize God in terms acceptable to ordinary discourse. Of course, Augustine said that any God that human beings might be able to understand certainly *cannot* be God. The triune nature of God strains understanding if it is expressed as an abstract argument, as though it could be reasoned out philosophically. The Christian doctrine of the Holy Trinity is rooted not as the product of a kind of theorizing, but in the experience of faithful people.

In Christian experience, God never stops being the immortal Sovereign who rules the entire universe. We have always known God as one who hears our prayers wherever we are and however many we are. God never stops being in charge of the universe, even while we recognize God in Jesus of Nazareth, crucified and risen. God never stops being Sovereign of all things, even while at work shaking things up and storming our hearts by means of the Holy Spirit. For Christians, to say anything less of God is to say too little; and to say very much more is to say too much. Can God be Sovereign of the universe, and at the very same time be incarnate in Jesus Christ? And, at the same time, be the active, vital, seeking, uniting Spirit? God is God's own interpreter, and we honor what we have received.

It is the communal and reflective experience of the church that has caused Christians, in all faithfulness, to speak of God as God has made the divine self known to us: as Father, Son, and Holy Spirit. The holy and blessed Trinity is not a problem to be solved, but a mystery. There is a difference. A problem is something that requires that we get to the bottom of it. A mystery is not something to be taken apart and resolved, but something to be pondered, lived with for a lifetime, handled with care, reverence, and humility.

The Muslims have my sympathy. Those who find themselves hung up on the arithmetic of one and three have my sympathy. The atheists have my sympathy. But the God who is Father, Son, and Holy Spirit lays claim to something else: my heart, and soul, and mind.

Is Preaching Trinitarian?

The Great Prayer of Thanksgiving is Trinitarian through and through, just as is the received faith of the church. Contemporary preaching, however, is not always as clearly Trinitarian. God may certainly be mentioned in preaching, but often it seems as though God plays the role of a distant reference, someone whose authority is invoked but who is not inclined to make a personal appearance. ("And now, a word from our sponsor!")

It is safe to call upon Jesus as a teacher, an ethicist, a social critic, and maybe sometimes a moralizer, while ducking stories from him or about him that strain credulity. The Holy Spirit can seem just nebulous enough to cover the churchly bases without obligating the preacher to address any fine points about a triune God.

"Triune God" sometimes gets a mention in sermons, without usually lingering over the "triune" part, and may be useful for the purpose of avoiding language that appears not to be gender inclusive. Is this judgment too broad, too much of a generalization? It may be, and probably it is—but we live in an era in which the preacher may feel at risk, ironically, by pressing congregations to think more deeply about God than has come to be expected in church.

Eucharistic prayer, if not circumvented by omissions or substitutions, sets before both congregation and preacher the God characterized in the New Testament as Father, Son, and Holy Spirit. God, of course, is greater than all our names for God. God is neither male nor female, neither parent nor child in any literal way. Nor is God a person hiding in the sky, sort of like the pathetic little man behind the scenes that the Wizard of Oz turns out to be. God is far more than a person—and yet, God is *at least* a person. Scripture gives us many images for God—some of them are impersonal: God is a rock, or a fortress. Some are feminine: God who bends down to nurse her children, God the woman searching for a lost coin. Some images of God borrow qualities from non-human creatures: God is like the eagle, bearing us up on her wings. But Scripture also gives us this name: Father, Son, Holy Spirit. This name is not good enough, not complete enough to say everything there might be to say about God. But it does say something essential. It says that God is not an "it." God is not "the force." God is not an impersonal field of energy. Whatever else God is, God is capable of entering into relationship. And so Scripture borrows relationship language, inadequate as it may be, but necessarily—Father, Son.

Scripture points to a divine strength at the very heart of God that is sufficient to watch over us—powerful enough to go head-to-head with the forces that threaten to pull the rug out from under us. And, at the very same time, at the very heart of God can be discerned One who crouched in the manger, who walks beside us as long as the journey takes, and who hangs with us when we come to the cross-shaped places. And, at the same time, at the very heart of God is Holy Spirit—a combination of strength and tenderness that breaks old boundaries and softens hardened hearts and makes communities out of strangers. It's because we know the one God in these three ways that we cannot be satisfied with speaking of God in any way that overlooks that threeness. Threeness, yes—but not three gods. Threeness, tri-unity, the self-identification of the one and only God there is. And in that tri-unity, relationship, and an invitation to relationship. Thus relational language: Father, Son, Holy Spirit.

In the first "person" of the Trinity, we catch a glimpse of the great God, the fountain from which flows everything that is and ever will be—the God whose quality of strength is sufficient to bring order out of chaos. The first person of the Trinity describes the God above us, the creator God, the God who is a sheltering mother, God the protecting Father.

Christ is God drawn near to us. Christ is our truth—not a doctrine, not an idea, not an explanation. Our truth is Christ, a living person, who is lifted up on the cross to take a place where the most vulnerable may find themselves; who descends into hell to preach good news to the spirits in prison (1 Pet 3:19). Our Christ, our truth, is the One who enters into the very depths of human suffering, because that is where he finds us. He finds us in those places where the people in charge lord it over us. He finds us in those places where powerful armies mow us down. He finds us in those places where we are beside ourselves, out of our right minds. He finds us in those places where we're bent over with crippling illness. He finds us in those places where we're shunned, ostracized, despised, cut off from the community. He finds us in those places where our own bitter choices have left us ashamed and out of options. He finds us in those places where we cannot even understand how or why we got there. The Christ of the heavy cross, the Christ of the empty cross, is the truth; and this Christ is not a second deity, but the one God as "second person" of the Trinity.

The Spirit is both comforter and disturber. The Spirit breaks down our pretensions, demonstrates with powerful clarity that we are not in control. The Spirit creates new things from scratch, compensates us for our losses, consoles us in our grief as we let go what must be let go. Left to ourselves, some of us would rearrange the furniture endlessly, pursue change for every reason and for no reason, leave nothing settled, undisturbed. Left to ourselves, others of us would change nothing, nail everything down, resist any suggestion that there might be delight in freshness. The Spirit challenges both. The Spirit values both old and new. Again, the God whom we perceive in the work of the Spirit is not a third deity, but the one God, the "third person" of the Trinity.

In recent years, in search of gender-inclusive language, one occasionally hears the Trinity named as Creator, Redeemer, and Sustainer. Besides this being a list of impersonal functions, it overlooks the fact that Scripture attributes all three of these functions to each of the three persons of the Trinity. See, for example, John 1:1–3; Heb 1:2–3; Pss 78:35; and 104:30.[1]

It is in this name we baptize: the Father who holds all things together, the Son who walks alongside us even in the places of terror and loss, and the Spirit who breaks down and builds up, who delivers to us intimate acquaintance with the Father and the Son. This is one God in three, three in one: Holy Trinity. One God, who in each of the three "persons" creates, redeems, and sustains.

Three Movements in Eucharistic Prayer

The West Syrian (Antiochene) form of eucharistic prayer is, like the ecumenical creeds, Trinitarian in its structure. The prayer has three movements, one focused on the first person of the Trinity, the next on the second person, and finally, the third person. One hears of an old saying, *Lex orandi, lex credendi*. It means, roughly, "The rule of what is prayed is the rule of what is believed." In other words, worship and theology are intimately related. In fact, whatever the form a liturgy may take, it embodies and projects a theology, whether the theology intended by the worship planners, or one not intended. Presuming that the considered theology of a church body is intentionally Trinitarian, that theology cries out to be embedded throughout the whole service, including preaching. It is this God and no other whom we praise, to whom we pray, and whom we proclaim. A preacher might do well to match public preaching and praying with the Trinitarian witness of the Great Thanksgiving. Begin, perhaps, with an effort to internalize the basic tripartite structure of the prayer, in which the church's Trinitarian faith is embedded.

Traveling with a group to visit the Russian Orthodox Church, our mostly clergy interdenominational group wanted to celebrate the Lord's Supper in our hotel in Moscow, since we were not able to commune in the churches we were visiting. No one was carrying a service book from any denomination, but most of those present knew the Antiochene form and content of the prayer, common in the revised service books of most mainline bodies, well enough to pray it without a written text. Apart from unusual experiences like that one, some congregations are committed to praying that, although it may have been thought through in advance, is offered without reading from a printed text and has about it some air of

---

1. See Byars, *Sacraments*, 132–33.

spontaneity, even though it honors the traditional shape and contents of eucharistic prayer. Guidelines for one preparing to offer eucharistic prayer in a free style can do it by learning these norms:

The prayer begins with thankful praise to God

for God's work in creation and providence, and in covenant history;

for the witness of the prophets;

for God's steadfast love in spite of human failure;

for the ultimate gift of Christ;

and for the immediate occasion or festival.

The prayer continues with thankful recalling of the acts of salvation in Jesus Christ:

Christ's birth, life, and ministry;

Christ's death and resurrection;

his present intercession for us and the promise of his coming again;

the gift of the sacrament [which may include the words of institution if not otherwise used.]

The Holy Spirit is called upon

to lift all who share the feast into Christ's presence;

to make the breaking of the bread and sharing of the cup a participation in the body and blood of Christ;

to make us one with the risen Christ and with all of God's people;

to unite us in communion with all the faithful in heaven and earth;

to nourish us with the body of Christ so that we may mature into the fullness of Christ;

to keep us faithful as Christ's body, representing Christ in ministry in the world, in anticipation of the fulfillment of the kingdom Christ proclaimed."[2]

Whether using a printed text or a free style, the prayer need not be as long as it would seem to be from the description above, which, even if it

---

2. Presbyterian Church (USA), "Great Thanksgiving 2," 122–23. Used by permission of Westminster John Knox Press.

were to be read aloud (neither recommended or intended!), is not as long as it looks in print. The risk of a free style is that important elements of the prayer may be left out when done from memory, either from not knowing which parts of the prayer are basic to it, or from ordinary forgetfulness. The Trinitarian form is essential. It is a single prayer, not three strung together, but in summary it looks like this.

A. thanksgiving to almighty God;

B. thanksgiving for Jesus Christ, including the expectation of his *parousia*;

C. calling upon the Holy Spirit, including a prayer for the communion of saints and anticipation of the reign of Christ.

The prayer concludes with a Trinitarian ascription of praise, followed by the people's "Amen," sung or said, and then the Lord's Prayer as a kind of summation.

Bible and Theology in Condensed Form

Gail Ramshaw describes the Great Thanksgiving as "the essential Christian faith in condensed format."[3] One could put together a whole course on theology using the eucharistic prayer as the basic outline. Or one could create a year-long study of the Bible. Part A, as I have described it for the sake of convenience, focusing on the first person of the Trinity, could serve as a format for a class on the Old Testament, of which the first movement of the Great Thanksgiving is mostly an abbreviated summary.

The *United Methodist Book of Worship* follows the basic ecumenical form derived from the Antiochene model. The opening dialogue exchanged by the presider and the worshiping assembly is the one that has become the historical and ecumenical norm:

> The Lord be with you.
> *And also with you.*
> Lift up your hearts.
> *We lift them to the Lord.*
> Let us give thanks to the Lord our God.
> *It is right to give our thanks and praise.*

---

3. Ramshaw, "Long and Short of Eucharistic Praying," 33.

The United Methodist example of what I am calling part A is the first movement of a eucharistic prayer intended for Advent. Note that the tone of the entire prayer is one of thanksgiving, and the theme of gratitude begins with the creation itself—the whole of the creation, "heaven and earth," both that part of the creation with which we are familiar and that part that is invisible to us but no less real.

> It is right, and a good and joyful thing, always and everywhere to give thanks to you, Father Almighty (*almighty God*), creator of heaven and earth. You formed us in your image and breathed into us the breath of life. When we turned away, and our love failed, your love remained steadfast. You delivered us from captivity, made covenant to be our sovereign God, and spoke to us through your prophets, who looked for that day when justice shall roll down like waters and righteousness like an ever-flowing stream, when nation shall not lift up sword against nation, neither shall they learn war any more.[4]

The book of Genesis, of course, testifies to the creation and its creator, beginning with the very first verse:

> In the beginning, when God created the heavens and the earth, the earth was a formless void and darkness covered the face of the deep, while a wind from God swept over the face of the waters. (Gen 1:1)

The two side-by-side creation stories in Gen 1 and 2 are represented in the second sentence of the prayer, "*You formed us in your image and breathed into us the breath of life*" (Gen 1:26–27; 2:7). The reference to "*our love failed*" is exemplified in the post-creation stories in the book of Genesis: the failure of the first two human beings in the garden of Eden (Gen 3); Cain murdering his brother Abel (Gen 4); God's disgust with "the wickedness of humankind" that leads to the flood (Gen 6); and God's love remaining *steadfast* as seen in the rainbow sign of the covenant established after the flood (6:18). Steadfast love continues to be represented in the story of a new thing, the "choosing" of a priestly people, beginning with ancestors Abraham and Sarah, including the story of their visitation by three strangers by the oaks of Mamre, bringing the promise that the aged couple would have a son (Gen 18:14–15), and God's promise to them that "by your offspring shall all the nations of the earth bless themselves" (Gen 22:18). If

---

4. *United Methodist Book of Worship*, 54.

you should decide to preach a sermon on the new beginning signaled in the promise to Sarah and Abraham, the Genesis text might lead you to reflect on it something like this:

A Preacher's Reflections: God's Encounters with Human Beings Are Always Resistant to Simple Explanation

All sorts of folks use the word "God" so easily, with so little care, as though everyone means the same thing by it, when actually, we don't. It is as though there were no mystery here, nothing hidden, God and everything about God as transparent and easily knowable as whoever is on the cover of this week's *People* magazine. The Bible has a great deal to say about God, but beneath all the revealing words the mystery remains. God's encounters with human beings are always veiled, always ambiguous, always resistant to simple explanation.

For example: Abraham, the spiritual ancestor common to Jews, Christians, and Muslims, was sitting at the entrance of his tent "in the heat of the day." Fanning himself, a jug of cool water within reach, he dozed in the heat. He saw no one coming, heard no one approach. All at once, "He looked up to see three men standing near him" (Gen 18:2a). *Three* visitors. Odd. Because the biblical account actually begins with these words: "*The* LORD appeared to Abraham by the oaks of Mamre, as he sat at the entrance of his tent." Who appeared? "*The* LORD—(*YHWH*, actually, the holy name of God in Hebrew)—appeared." But what Abraham saw, standing before him, was three men.

Abraham rises to the occasion. He goes on automatic pilot. He doesn't have to think about what to do, because in his culture the default setting is to offer hospitality to strangers. He addresses the three saying, "My lord" (small letter "l")—"My lord [singular] . . . Let a little water be brought, and wash your feet, and rest yourselves [plural] under the tree" (18:3).

In Exodus, God said to Moses, "no one shall see me and live" (Exod 33:20). Whenever the Bible records an encounter between God and a human being, God always manages to remain a step removed. Sometimes God is hidden in an intermediary, often an "angel." (The Bible nowhere systematically defines what an angel is, but in reading about an angelic messenger, it's not always easy to tell whether the angel is God, or an intermediary, or both at the same time.)

You'd prefer a simple explanation? Something straightforward, unambiguous, spelled out in sharp clarity, like the current temperature flashing in color on the front of your bank? It doesn't work that way. God is too big for any human mind even to begin to comprehend. And any deity that we *can* comprehend is surely *not* God.

Many of us have imagined that we would like to have a direct encounter with God, one that would end our doubts and uncertainties once and for all. Although, it is unlikely that we would be able to survive it. "No one shall see me and live." But God finds other means of speaking to us. In a quote popularly attributed to Malcolm Muggeridge, he says, "Every happening, great or small, is a parable whereby God speaks to us; the art of life is to get the message." Not many of us are likely to have an encounter with God that resembles Abraham's, or the ones Moses had, or Joseph's or Mary's angelic visitations. But it is well to note that, as Muggeridge observed, "Every happening, great or small, is a parable whereby God speaks to us." *Every* happening, great or small. And yet, it is risky to interpret any parabolic message all by oneself. Better to submit it to communal reflection with other people of faith.

How do we, together in these days, understand the commonplace parables working themselves out right now? What is God doing? Saying? To us and for us? What's God saying in a time when the default setting for faith has shifted: a time in which it's easier not to believe in God, not to trust what anybody says about God? And, how might God choose to speak to us in a time of political and religious polarization? A time when old, often buried, questions about race, and tribe, and nation, questions about what the richest and the poorest may owe each other, have forced us to explore beyond our comfort zone?

Abraham, knowing it was the pious thing to do, snapped to attention and began to organize a meal for his unexpected guests. Now, you might think that a pitcher of water and a tuna sandwich might have been sufficient on a hot day, or maybe a big pasta salad and a glass of iced tea. But no, he organizes what's going to be something more like Christmas dinner. Abraham sticks his head into the kitchen and tells Sarah to fire up the oven. Abraham picked a calf out of the herd and told his servant how to prepare it, and when everything was ready, he served the food himself. "And he stood by them under the tree while they ate" (18:8b).

During the meal, "They said to him, 'Where is your wife Sarah?'" (18:9a). How did they know Sarah's name? I doubt, in that culture, that any introduction had been made. And then, more surprisingly, one of them declares that he intends to visit again, after a time, "and your wife Sarah shall have a son" (18:10). How did he know that Sarah grieved over her childlessness? Sarah was heard laughing, and then the LORD (*YHWH* in the text) said, "Is anything too wonderful for the LORD?" (Again, *YHWH*.) The narrator and those who handed on the story seem not to have been uneasy about the moves that treat three visiting men as, at the same time, a single, divine visitor. The ambiguity is embedded in the fact that it is not always clear when we are dealing with God in some apparently ordinary encounter.

The story of the three visitors is a story remembered, evaluated, pondered retrospectively, after the fact. It is a naïve story that is profound at the same time. The Hebrew people cherished the story, because it is meant to interpret their own origins theologically: i.e., in reference to their God. Abraham and Sarah were, of course, blessed by a son in their old age, just as promised (Exod 21:5). They named him Isaac. Isaac produced his own sons, one of whom was named Jacob, but Jacob was also called by the name "Israel" (Exod 25:26; 32:28). And Jacob/Israel was the father of twelve sons of his own, the heads of the twelve tribes who became the people of Israel. So the promise: "Your wife Sarah shall have a son"—however unlikely—was a promise kept. Out of barrenness, God had created a people. Created a people both blessed and burdened by a special task—to serve God in a world that would just as soon not hear anything about this God or any claims this God might make upon them. And out of this people, formed from the union of Sarah and Abraham, would come the Christ, who stretches out his arms to everybody—Galileans, Samaritans, gentiles, atheists, fundamentalists, Rastafarians, psychiatrists, and even mainline Christians.

"Every happening, great or small, is a parable whereby God speaks to us; the art of life is to get the message." The message was communicated to Abraham and Sarah, whether with or without words—how can we really know? The message was communicated in, under, and with the meal eaten under the oaks of Mamre. And the heart of the message was a promise that the future belongs to God—and God would see them through.

It is no wonder that God should have communicated the divine promise in and along with a meal. When we eat together, we let our guard down. We find ourselves opening up, even if only a little, to those with whom we share the meal. We become present to one another in ways that are rare in other settings.

Is it so surprising, then, that the Lord Jesus took bread, gave thanks, broke it, and gave it to his disciples both on the night when he was betrayed and at table in Emmaus on Easter evening after he was raised? Is it so surprising that the Lord Jesus gave us a meal, and the promise of his presence in it, that we may not just hear, but actually eat and drink the sacred promise? That we might digest and internalize the promise that the Holy God will stand by us, and see us through, even when it seems impossible? Even when all the familiar landmarks have been moved almost overnight?

Three visitors sat down to eat. And yet, hidden in and among the three was "the Lord," Yahweh, whom no one can encounter directly and live. "The Lord" was Abraham's guest, Sarah's guest. And yet, the Lord was also the host—the One who fed Sarah and her husband with a promise, even though they were not yet equipped to digest it. And so with us: the Lord is both guest and host at the meal that's been prepared for us. And it's the Lord—the Lord about whom we could say little of any use at all were it not for God's self-disclosure in Jesus Christ—it's the Lord—both guest and host—who nourishes us with a promise revealed in food and drink: "The future is mine," says the Lord. "I will be with you."

Theological Affirmations in the Form of Stories

The Abraham and Sarah story continues as it moves on to stories of their progeny: Isaac, the promise made good, and Isaac's son Jacob and his family, including the saga of Jacob's lost son, Joseph, ultimately reconciling with his brothers in Egypt.

Genesis, along with much of the Bible, makes theological affirmations using the medium of stories, in which the character of God and God's relationship with human beings are embodied in the narratives rather than in discursive explanations. This is not objective history, as understood from the point of view of Enlightenment rationalism. The stories are not recorded as academic historians might do it, but rather told artistically, fashioned for the purpose of giving a glimpse of what cannot be seen: i.e., God's hand at work among human beings who bear all the promise and the limitations that are stubbornly characteristic of all of us, now as well as then.

The United Methodist Thanksgiving continues, God "delivered us from captivity, *made covenant* to be our sovereign." For example, after the exodus from captivity in Egypt, when the Hebrew people had reached the land of promise, Joshua urged them to "choose this day whom you will serve . . . as for me and my household, we will serve the LORD," and the people vowed to do the same. "So Joshua made a covenant with the people that day"—a covenant in which God is sovereign (Josh 24:15, 25).

Of course Israel later suffered from a calamitous second captivity in the time of Jeremiah, when the Chaldeans sacked Jerusalem and marched all the most prominent people to exile in Babylon. When the Persian King Cyrus finally released them, decades later, the liberation was celebrated as a providential act of God. "In the first year of King Cyrus of Persia, in order that the word of the Lord by the mouth of Jeremiah might be accomplished" (Ezra 1:1). The returned exiles gathered in Jerusalem to hear the priest Ezra read aloud forgotten words from the Torah to an assembly of the recently liberated, and "the people wept when they heard the words of the law" (Neh 8:9), clearly another instance of covenant renewal. Is such a renewal possible for us?

A Preacher's Reflections: The Prophets: Whose Side Are They On?

The first movement of this United Methodist Great Thanksgiving honors the God who "*spoke to us through your prophets,*" "*who looked for that day when justice shall roll down like waters and righteousness like an ever-flowing stream,*" a direct quote from Amos 5:24, and "*when nation shall not lift up sword against nation, neither shall they learn war any more*" (Isa 2:4). These quotes bear an eschatological imperative. The reign of God will not be entirely realized until the *parousia* ("second coming"), but we can imagine something of what it will look like, and it has a shape that guides our communal lives of faith even now. The prophets engaged in risky speech, calling out those in positions of power who scorned the weak and neglected justice for the vulnerable.

Amos was not a professional prophet. He left off raising sheep and began to do some public speaking. At first, his audiences loved it. Amos spoke of God's impatience with Israel's neighboring nations. He said that God was going to cast judgment on Damascus. Then he promised that God was going to hold to account the people of Gaza, and Tyre, and the folks in Edom, Ammon, Moab, and Judah. Amos's audiences were thrilled! They cheered him on, begged to hear more. But then Amos dropped a bombshell. As he listed all the peoples God was going to judge, he added one more: Israel (the northern kingdom, where his audience lived). At that point, the applause abruptly halted. The crowds went silent.

Amos went on to compare Israel to a basket of summer fruit. The fruit is ripe and juicy in the summer, but when summer is over, it begins to rot. And that, said Amos, is the destiny of their homeland, Israel. Amos handed on a word from God:

> The end has come upon my people Israel. . . . Songs of the temple shall become wailings in that day . . . the dead bodies shall be many, cast out in every place. (Amos 8:2b–3)

What was going on here? Why had God found fault with Israel? Amos quickly became painfully specific. He accuses Israel of having become deceived by its own peace and prosperity. They have become smug and complacent. They have sunk into a kind of moral coma. They have lost track of the values in which God had so carefully tutored them by means of Torah and earlier prophets. Amos cries out in God's name, "Hear this, you that trample on the needy, and bring to ruin the poor of the land" (8:4). He accuses them of having become so obsessed with making money that everything else has taken a back seat. They can't stand to close their shops for the holy days; they can't stand to let their employees off for one day a week—because nothing is as important to them as piling up profits. Amos mimics them: "When will the new moon be over so that we may sell grain; and the sabbath, so that we may offer wheat for sale?" (8:5).

The prophet accuses them of cheating their customers; there are thumbs on the scales. They sell inferior products. They "practice deceit with false balances, buying the poor for silver and the needy for a pair of sandals, and selling the sweepings of the wheat" (8:6). They take advantage of people who are not in a position to look after their own interests. Amos delivers God's condemnation: "Surely I will never forget any of their deeds . . . I will turn your feasts into mourning, and all your songs into lamentations" (8:7b, 10a).

Are we twenty-first-century folks to assume, then, that God is antibusiness? Hostile to making a profit? Is God the leader of some kind of fanatical consumer movement? There is no evidence that God is hostile to business. God is not forbidding commerce or profit making. What God is doing is to promise that there is hell to be paid for widespread dishonesty, and particularly for dishonest business practices that exploit the poor, the weak, and the vulnerable. But more than that, God is accusing a whole society of having lost its bearings. They have become obsessed with—what?—the bottom line? Guaranteeing their own security? Winning the economic game no matter what it takes?

Moneymaking had smothered every other human enterprise. It was not possible to enjoy a holiday, because the merchants were champing at the bit to get it over with and open the markets again. There was no enjoyment of Sabbath rest, because that one-day-in-seven got in the way of ringing up sales. It was not just a matter of excessive zeal for doing business. It was a matter of distorting human life, spoiling human community. This obsession dwarfed every other human enterprise: worship, of course, but also simple leisure, music, art, friendship. The obsession with money had squashed every other value, made it all contemptible.

God, speaking through Amos, declared in non-negotiable language that any society that neglects or exploits the weak and vulnerable will surely perish—if not in the short run, then certainly in the long run. Repeatedly, Amos identifies the victims of the northern kingdom's distorted values: "the needy," he cries; the "needy," and "the poor of the land." It may be acceptable to look out for number one as long as that does not require neglecting the interests of the community as a whole. Amos has accused Israel of exactly that kind of neglect. Those who hold economic power in their hands have ravished the community. For all practical purposes, they have plundered the weak and left them beaten and half dead in the marketplace. "I will turn your feasts into mourning," God promised. "I will make it like the mourning for an only son" (8:10b).

If Amos were a figure often quoted in today's media, I can imagine a CNN panel discussing his work. The moderator might ask a consultant psychiatrist what she thinks causes Amos to attack the integrity of free-market society so intensely. Her answer might be, "Well, it is rumored that Amos grew up in a working class family, one of seven children. Amos had to make do with whatever clothes they could round up, and the other kids frequently made fun of his hand-me-downs. He brought his teacher an orange at Christmas, while all the others brought wrapped gifts. I suspect," the therapist suggests, "that Amos's anger is rooted in early trauma when classmates from well-to-do households belittled him mercilessly."

The next consultant on the panel is an economist, who insists that Amos's anger flows from the fact that he really does not understand the dynamics of contemporary economics, particularly the trickle-down theory. A newly elected member of Congress speaks next, and she thinks that Amos was influenced by left-wing professors when he was at university.

A law professor believes that Amos has violated the conventions requiring separation of church and state; and a local pastor believes that Amos has overreacted, and been insensitive to the needs and anxieties of hardworking and well-meaning members of the business community (who also deserved credit for being generous with their churches). If there had been a vote on whether the book of Amos should have a place in Scripture, his own generation would have voted against it. And so would our own.

It is commonplace to dismiss the God of the Old Testament as a God of judgment, as though judgment were a primitive notion, now grown obsolete. It is equally commonplace to believe that the God of the New Testament loves everybody indiscriminately: saint as well as sinner. So, why bother to be a saint? There is something wrong with this picture. What does love look like, anyway?

A parent has two teenagers. One always has the car home on time and it is clean and in good condition. The other has had three accidents in a year, never meets a curfew, and always brings the car home with a nearly empty gas tank and a stray beer can or two under the seat. The parent loves both equally. Does that mean that the parent hands over the car keys as readily to one as to the other? Is that what love means? Or, might love require the parent to set different rules for the careless child? Does the child who gets grounded feel loved? Or judged? Apart from what the child feels, is it possible to see love exhibited in the parents' judgment?

A full-blown biblical view of God is this: that God may very well exercise the most profound love through actions that feel like rejection. God may demonstrate persistent caring by drawing a line not to be crossed. God's wrath may conceal a love that just won't quit. God deals with destructive behaviors as vigorously as those behaviors may require. Those whom God chastens may feel rejected, but in fact the chastening is God's way of refusing to let go of us. It is for our own sakes that God is not going to look away or just obliterate us while we are exploiting the weak or dismissing their interests through our indifference.

The prophets' frequent calls for justice—not the least of which was economic justice—was meant to address the inequities of the moment, and so it was, after all, not only a theological issue but also systemic—even political. Neither the rulers, religious leaders or (false) prophets were spared:

> Hear this, you rulers of the house of Jacob and chiefs of the house of Israel, who abhor justice and pervert all equity, who build Zion with blood and Jerusalem with wrong! Its rulers give judgment for

a bribe, its priests teach for a price, its prophets give oracles for money; yet they lean upon the LORD and say, "Surely the LORD is with us! No harm shall come upon us." (Mic 3:9–11)

A Prophetic Vision: The Basileia

The prophetic word often points to the *basileia*: "But the earth will be filled with the knowledge of the glory of the LORD, as the waters cover the sea," in the words of the prophet Habbakuk (2:14). Zechariah foresees an eschatological moment when

> Old men and old women shall again sit in the streets of Jerusalem, each with staff in hand because of their great age. And the streets of the city shall be full of boys and girls playing in its streets. (Zech 8:4)

Justice will characterize the *basileia*, even though justice is elusive in our own time, however much we may long for it. Justice, then, is a recurring eschatological theme. So are both peace and the crossing of boundaries—an astonishing inclusiveness that extends even to bitter enemies.

> On that day Israel will be the third with Egypt and Assyria, a blessing in the midst of the earth, whom the Lord of hosts has blessed, saying, "Blessed be Egypt my people, and Assyria the work of my hands, and Israel my heritage." (Isa 19:24–25)

A Lutheran version of part A of the eucharistic prayer echoes the one cited from *The United Methodist Book of Worship.*

> We thank you for the new world to come and for the love that will rule all in all. We praise you for the grace shown to Israel, your chosen, the people of your promise: the rescue from Egypt, the gift of the promised land, the memory of the fathers, the homecoming from exile, and the prophets' words that will not be in vain.[5]

An eschatological reference is evident in the thanksgiving *"for the new world to come and for the love that will rule all in all,"* as is the affirmation that *"the prophets' words will not be in vain."* Even the references to *"the promised land"* and *"homecoming from exile"* may be understood eschatologically, as they both also serve as metaphors for the *basileia*.

---

5. Lutheran Church in America, *Lutheran Book of Worship*, 221.

The Great Thanksgiving: An Invitation to Preach the Things at the Center

Those in the congregation who are familiar with the shorthand biblical references will recognize them in the eucharistic prayer with no difficulty. Those who do not, and there are many such in this era of reduced biblical literacy, will not. For the prayer to be prayerfully embraced, in fact, by the worshiping congregation, it will be useful to teach its structure and its content to the people. What some identify as our post-establishment situation calls for new efforts in intentional catechesis even of existing constituencies.

What once had been naively taken more or less for granted can no longer simply be presumed to have taken place sometime, somehow. The teaching ministry of the church might make use of examples from eucharistic prayer with the specific purpose of familiarizing the people with biblical context and content and with basic ecumenical theology. This may be done in classes specifically for such a purpose—teaching occasions outside of worship, perhaps around a meal, or even in small, personalized face-to-face settings. One can imagine, particularly during that long part of the liturgical year between Trinity Sunday and Christ the King, preaching a series based on some of the textual references made or alluded to in the Great Thanksgiving. Certainly, the eucharistic prayer itself can serve to remind the preacher not to neglect engagement with these Scriptures evoked directly or indirectly in liturgical prayer. They are basic to the Christian vision of God's identity and God's purposes, both for here and now, and ultimately, in the *basileia* that even now presses upon us a sense of what God desires for us and from us in our own time.

The Great Thanksgiving Is Doxological: Praise from Beginning to End

The tripartite eucharistic prayer invites the congregation to add their voices in transitions that lead from part A to part B, and then again after part B to part C, normally sung, but sometimes said. The responses at intervals help to engage the congregation, and assist in their tracing of the course of the tripartite prayer, and to discern the particular accents of each of its three parts.

The old Latin name for the first transition, leading from part A to part B, is the *Sanctus* followed by and linked to the *Benedictus*. The form of the *Sanctus* most widely used is:

> Holy, holy, holy Lord,
> God of power and might,
> heaven and earth are full of your glory,
> Hosanna in the highest.[6]

Some churches, such as the United Church of Christ, have slightly altered the wording for purposes of accenting gender inclusivity:

> Holy, holy, holy God
> of love and majesty,
> the whole universe speaks of your glory,
> O God Most High.[7]

The *Sanctus* derives from Isaiah, with a vision of "the Lord sitting on a throne, high and lofty":

> Holy, holy, holy is the Lord of hosts;
>   the whole earth is full of his glory. (Isa 6:3)

The *Benedictus*:

> Blessed is he who comes in the name of the Lord.
>   Hosanna in the highest. (Ps 118:26)

Some churches, such as the UCC, change the "he" to "the one" who comes in the name of the Lord. "Hosanna" is not part of the Psalm, but drawn from the New Testament story of Jesus' triumphal entry into Jerusalem in all three synoptic Gospels (Matt 21:9; Mark 11:9; Luke 19:38; John 12:13).

---

6. Church of Scotland, *Book of Common Order*, 133.
7. *Book of Worship: United Church of Christ*, 46.

6

Christological Preaching

The Grace of the Lord Jesus Christ . . .

THE SECOND MOVEMENT OF the Great Thanksgiving, which I am labeling as part B, is normally called the *anamnesis*, Greek for *reminder* or *remembrance*. It segues from and expands an expression of gratitude for Jesus Christ with which part A concludes briefly. The *anamnesis* normally includes the words of institution, except for those churches that continue to follow Calvin's practice of using them before or after the prayer. An *anamnesis* for use in the Presbyterian Church of Canada follows the *Sanctus* and *Benedictus* sung or said as a transition leading from part A to part B:

> We praise you, most holy God, for sending your only Son Jesus to live among us, full of grace and truth. Sharing our joy and sorrow, he healed the sick and was a friend of sinners. Obeying you, he took up his cross and died that we might live. We praise you that he overcame death and is risen to rule the world. He is still the friend of sinners. We trust him to overcome every power that can hurt or divide us, and believe that when he comes in glory we will celebrate victory with him.
>
> [Here follow words of institution, in a paraphrase not identical to any one of the Gospel narratives.]
>
> Therefore, in remembrance of your mighty acts in Jesus Christ, we take this bread and this cup and give you praise and thanksgiving as we proclaim the mystery of faith.[1]

---

1. Presbyterian Church in Canada, *Book of Common Worship*, 83–84.

CHRISTOLOGICAL PREACHING

A Preacher's Reflections: Jesus' Ministry as a Down Payment

"Sharing our joy and sorrow, he healed the sick."

One wonders, sometimes, what good Jesus' healings did? It was lifesaving for those he met, and upon whom he laid hands, and to whom he restored wholeness. But what good does it do those who have to bear their afflictions without such relief? If an illness or injury doesn't yield to medical treatment, healing is elusive. Sometimes healing occurs on its own by way of medically recognized processes or simply unexplainably, but often not. It seems that the point of Jesus' ministry of healing might not have been merely to favor a few, but to flash up on the screen a preview of what God has in store for the whole creation. In that ultimate future, the repaired and restored creation that God is preparing for us, there will be no disfigurement, no deteriorating illness, no incapacitating depression, no lack of sight or hearing or speech or nimbleness of foot. Wherever Jesus went, God's rule touched down in the moment. Those with the sensitivity to see it caught a glimpse of what it will be like for everybody when God's *basileia* is made manifest.

"God's got a lot of explaining to do"

For centuries people have speculated about where evil comes from. Why is the world as broken as it is? In Anne Tyler's novel, *A Patchwork Planet*, a young man works for a company called "Rent-a-Back."[2] If you need someone to put up a Christmas tree, or shop for groceries, or clean out your garage, you just call Rent-a-Back, and they send someone out to do it. Not surprisingly, most of the company's clients are elderly people. One such customer is Maud May. She is a pretty tough character, and has managed to stay independent for a long time. But now she has just come home after a stay in the hospital, and she is feeling uncharacteristically feeble. She gets into a conversation with one of the employees of Rent-a-Back. He reports it for the reader.

"'In the afterlife,' Maud May told me, 'God's got a lot of explaining to do.'" 'What about?' I asked. I was unpacking groceries, and she was smoking a cigarette at her kitchen table. 'Oh,' she said, 'children suffering, cancer, tidal waves, tornadoes . . .' The Rent-a-back fellow replies, 'You think those

2. Tyler, *Patchwork Planet*, 266.

need explaining? Tornadoes just happen, man. You think God sits around aiming tornadoes at people on purpose?' Maud May continues, unfazed. 'Old ladies breaking their hips and becoming a burden...' The Rent-a-Back man answers, 'The most He might explain is how to deal with a tornado... How to accept it or endure it or whatever; how to do things right. That's what I'm going to ask about when I get to heaven myself: how to do things right.'"

We don't know why this beautiful, wonderful world is as twisted and broken as it is. We don't know why there have to be devastating natural disasters, World Wars, or terrorists or people who go around bent over for eighteen years, like the poor woman Jesus healed on a Sabbath (Luke 13:10-17). What God shows us in Jesus is that such misery is not what God wants for us. And in Jesus' ministry of healing, God declares that things are not going to stay this way. The whole creation—including you and me—is going to be liberated, restored to what it was meant to be.

In the meantime, before the *parousia*, Jesus continues to lay his hands on those whose lives have been disfigured. He equips us to deal with whatever we have to deal with. He heals the heart and soul, so that no bodily affliction can define us, or have the last word over us.

Jesus promises that "Satan's" power will be broken, and that the will of God shall be done on earth, as it is in heaven. That is why, even though we are well acquainted with the anguish of the world, the church nevertheless takes heart. "And the entire crowd was rejoicing at all the wonderful things that he was doing" (Luke 13:17b). The amazing things that occurred wherever Jesus went during his ministry serve as a down payment on the ultimate future God has in mind for us: the reign of God for which we pray every Sunday.

A Preacher's Reflections: The Cross

The *anamnesis* above, this second movement of the Great Thanksgiving in a Presbyterian Church of Canada version, continues to sum up Jesus' historical ministry among us, including *"Obeying you, he took up his cross and died that we might live."* The *anamnesis* from Rite II in the Episcopal *Book of Common Prayer* frames it like this: "*He stretched out his arms upon the cross, and offered himself in obedience to your will, a perfect sacrifice for the whole world.*"[3] The image of "stretching out his arms" not only indicates

---

3. Episcopal Church, *Book of Common Prayer*, 362.

the means of his death by crucifixion, but also suggests that from the cross he is opening his arms to embrace the whole world. Sometimes one may hear in a sermon that "Jesus died for our sins." Many members of congregations are familiar with that phrase, but would be hard-pressed to say what it means. The preacher would do well to think it through personally rather than simply repeating the formulaic words by rote. The goal would be to try to express "died for us" in the preacher's own words, keeping in mind the way people in a specific congregation are listening. As in Scripture itself, the sermon interprets the cross most effectively by way of narrative rather than by abstract reasoning.

A few years ago, a former colleague, who grew up in another country, reported seeing bumper stickers that read "God bless America." He said that he could not help but think that this was meant to be an imperative rather than a petition. Nor could he avoid the impression that it might imply an unwritten warning, perhaps something like "God bless America" . . . "*or—we'll get another god.*" In other words, when God seems friendly to our belief that we are and ought to be a favored people; that we are in some special way "exceptional," and that God will always take our side in any dispute with other nations, and that our virtue entitles us to special privilege—well, then, we are happy to honor this God. However, if God seems to fall down on the job—say, not come to the rescue when we continue to poison our own air and water, or not cause every conflict to be resolved in our favor, or, even worse, should confront us with our own many social, international, and personal culpabilities—then we shall certainly find ourselves in the market for a more obliging deity.

In other words, it is easy enough to make a place for God on the bumper sticker as long as God neither disappoints us nor confronts us nor calls us to see ourselves clearly and, yes, repent. But, most of the human race has experienced enough hardship, enough disappointment, enough failure, enough anguish to have stored up either a little or a lot of resentment towards whoever is in charge of the universe. And, given just the right moment, that resentment may come out as pure rage. That, I think, is one way of understanding the cross. Jesus represents the holy God in word, in action, and in person, the Word made flesh. However dimly his identity may be perceived, he becomes the victim when our rage against the universe seeks a target.

God created the world and called it good. Goodness is visible not only in the natural world, but in the human story. And yet, there is also violence.

Violence is a kind of contrapuntal theme, weaving itself in and out of all the melodies the world sings. And yet, we hide our eyes from violence. We deny it, are surprised when we encounter it, and try to protect ourselves from imagining it has anything to do with us, because the fact that there is random violence in the world disturbs our sense of order, of being in control of our own lives. The story of the human race is the story of wills in conflict. It begins as early as Adam and Eve in the garden of Eden, who defy God and clash with one another. The Old Testament tells story after story about these clashing wills: people against God, people against each other, and often enough, God apparently picking sides!

When Jesus leaves the upper room on the night of his betrayal and goes to the Garden of Gethsemane, it might serve as an alert for us to consider this second garden as a clue in the narrative. A garden may be the starting point for a great reversal, the potential undoing of what had been lost in Eden, the first garden. When the soldiers come to Gethsemane; when Jesus is scourged and insulted, sentenced and crucified, we again see wills in conflict. When Jesus hangs on the cross, the direction of punishment has clearly shifted. It is no longer God's punishment turned against the stubborn, as in the response to the first couple's rebellion, or in the days of Noah, or in the time of Pharoah's heedlessness that led to the loss of every one of Egypt's firstborn sons. On the cross, the punishment is directed from human beings into the very heart of God.

How can we shift our perceptions to see God not as a punishing, threatening, side-choosing deity, but One who voluntarily submits to the role of victim rather than One who makes victims: God the rejected, the crucified God? It would seem to mean that God, viewed cross-wise, reveals God's self not as present to the world in sheer power, forcibly subduing the stubborn; but rather God become present to the world in weakness, in vulnerability, in sharing with us the all-too-familiar status of victim. When there is a violent clash between human wills and God's will, in the cross God absorbs the fury. There will be no more divinely sent floods, no more punishing violence sent from heaven to scourge human beings, if ever there were. The God of the cross is present to us in our losses, present in our woundedness, present in our brokenness and in our disappointment. And maybe what has been revealed of God's character in the cross is the way the true God has been all along. Certainly, on the cross, we see that this is who God is.

Christological Preaching

We often hear that God has atoned for our sins by paying a kind of ransom. Although the familiarity of the payoff image would suggest that there is no other way to interpret the affirmation that "Jesus died for our sins," the fact is that paying a debt on our behalf is only one metaphor among several in the New Testament.

> God's reconciling act in Jesus Christ is a mystery which the Scriptures describe in various ways. It is called the sacrifice of a lamb, a shepherd's life given for the sheep, atonement by a priest; again it is ransom of a slave, payment of debt, vicarious satisfaction of legal penalty, and victory over the powers of evil. These are expressions of a truth which remains beyond the reach of all theory in the depths of God's love for [us]. They reveal the gravity, cost, and sure achievement of God's reconciling work.[4]

No single metaphor all by itself is likely to be sufficient when speaking of holy things. Usually two or more metaphors set alongside each other offer particular perspectives, each one expanding, limiting, critiquing the others. Nevertheless, it is evident that God's reaching out to us in Christ costs something. Every relationship costs something, of course: parent-child, spouse-spouse, friend-friend, etc. Ideally, one imagines that the cost of any relationship ought to be shared fifty-fifty, but in fact, that is rarely the case. Frequently, one of the persons in a relationship bears more of the cost than the other. It may be divided sixty-forty, twenty-eighty, or whatever. One party is likely to be more patient, more persistent, more giving, shouldering more of the burdens required to sustain a relationship.

In his book, *The Cost of Discipleship*, Dietrich Bonhoeffer wrote about something he called "cheap grace." What is "cheap grace"? Grace is "cheap" when we presume that forgiveness does not cost the forgiver anything. In the case of the gospel, "cheap grace" is to presume that forgiving my sins and those of the entire human race costs God nothing. Bonhoeffer knew, however, that while forgiveness may be free, it is never cheap.

In the cross, it is clear that it is God who pays the greater cost of a relationship with us, a cost that could not possibly be borne by any human being nor even all of us together. It is God who absorbs the rage, the indifference, the insults, the turned backs, the fingers pointed, the clever excuses that shift the blame away from ourselves and towards heaven. As we human beings pass the hot potato of our discontent from one to another looking for someone else to hold the blame for our grievances, endlessly

---

4. Presbyterian Church (USA), "Confession of 1967," 254.

redistributing our pain and anger, it eventually reaches the ruler of the universe, the crucified Shepherd. In the cross, the incarnate God does not pass it on one more time, as we do, or toss it back to us, as we might, but embraces the burning grievances we are so desperate to get off our hands. The cross is God choosing for the buck to stop right there, on that hill. It is God who takes the heat and absorbs the "cost." "Jesus died for our sins."

In the person of Jesus, God incarnate absorbs the disappointment and hostility of the whole human race; becomes the target of every rage ever displaced toward an authority figure. And what does God do with it? God in Christ takes the hostility, takes the rage, and transforms it, giving it back as bread and wine. God gives it back, not in the form of revenge, but in the form of nourishment. The God whom people so easily reproach, consciously or not, directly or indirectly, turns out to be the God who draws near to us in our belligerence and our despair, to feed us and strengthen us in body and soul. The God of the cross calls Christ's disciples to share, in some measure, the suffering servant's vulnerability. The God of the cross calls us to expose ourselves to the risks that accompany those who share the service of priestly intercession and advocacy. "But you are a chosen race, a royal priesthood . . . that you may proclaim the mighty acts of him who called you out of darkness into his marvelous light (1 Pet 2:9; see also Rev 1:6; 5:10).

A Preacher's Reflections: Resurrection

"We praise you that he overcame death and is risen to rule the world."

Easter poses a challenge—not just for people of a skeptical frame of mind—but a challenge as well for those who think of themselves as people of faith. On Easter Sunday, churches are likely to be filled with people who are of two minds: they want to believe, but there are lots of reasons not to. Want to believe, but, from childhood on, we accumulate a lot of experience believing in someone or something, only to be disillusioned, disappointed, let down. Our hearts pull us in one direction on Easter; sad experience causes us to remember how painful it is to find ourselves misled. "Lord, I believe; help my unbelief" (Mark 9:24).

Take, for example, the experience of disciples on Easter evening. They were afraid that the authorities who had caused Jesus to be crucified would come after them next. As John tells it, they were gathered on Sunday night behind locked doors, nervous and wary. We don't know what they had been saying or doing. But John reports that suddenly they sensed that something in the room had changed. One more person had been added to their number. Startled, they identified the unexpected newcomer as the crucified Jesus, his wounds clearly visible. He breathed on them, just as God had breathed life into the first human being, as recorded in Gen 2. He commissioned them to be agents of mercy, of forgiveness, of reconciliation. And then the visitation ended as mysteriously as it had begun.

One of the remaining eleven—Thomas—wasn't there. Maybe he was talking things out with a family member, or shopping for food, or just keeping his body moving to quiet his mind, the way you do when you go for a walk or a run. But when he came back to the locked place, the others told him of their experience. "But he said to them, 'Unless I see the mark of the nails in his hands, and put my finger in the mark of the nails and my hand in his side, I will not believe'" (John 20:25b). Who can blame Thomas? He wanted to believe, but it wasn't any easier then than it is now. "Lord, I believe; help my unbelief."

A whole week flies by, and John doesn't tell us anything about how disciples spent the seven days and nights. Now it is Sunday evening again, and the disciples are behind closed doors in the same place, but this time, Thomas is there. Once again, with no knock on the door, no key turning in the lock, Jesus becomes manifest in their midst. He greets them again saying, "Shalom," "Peace." But then he turns directly to Thomas, inviting him to touch his wounded hands and side.

So, if you were Thomas, would you say that you'd seen a ghost? After all, Jesus didn't seem to be shut out by closed doors. Or, touching the wounds, would you presume that Jesus was a resuscitated corpse? Or, was he neither ghost nor revitalized corpse, but a phenomenon utterly beyond any conceivable category?

Thomas has often been characterized as a "doubter," as though he suffered from a character flaw. But I don't see him as any different from you or me. He wanted to believe, all right. Who wouldn't? But he wanted to defend himself from cruel disappointment, too. So, he held back. He restrained himself. He wouldn't rush into anything.

Of course, we all know people who are perpetual doubters—people for whom doubt provides the basic shape of their lives; folks so disenchanted that they've shifted from reasonable skepticism to bitter cynicism. Maybe they once thought that people in high office, people in charge of institutions, people entrusted with power and authority actually behaved the way the social studies textbooks imply they ought to behave. That was before the indictment of the county sheriff; before the judge was removed; before the priest was accused, the teacher arrested, and the Congressman impeached. How easy it would be to grow utterly cynical, trusting no one, trusting no word from any authority, trusting nothing that purports to be good news. Cynicism.

But I don't think that's the case with Thomas. Rather, I'd like to think that Thomas is using doubt as a tool with which to dig deeper. That's how doubt works for people in the sciences; for historians; for sociologists; for journalists; for biblical scholars and theologians. Doubt doesn't have to be cynical. It can serve to test what we think we know. It can help us to see more than what's immediately apparent. It can open us to possibilities otherwise unimagined. It can give us a leg to stand on.

So, I don't have any quarrel with Thomas—although he may have longed for a level of certainty that one rarely, if ever, can lay hold of in this world. After all, even before Jesus' second appearance, Thomas already had the testimony of people he trusted. People whose lives were linked with his, people who had every bit as much at stake as he did should they be proven wrong.

And that, of course, is something like what you and I have, too. By baptism you and I have been embedded in a community whose roots are entwined with those disciples in that locked room on the first Easter evening. The Holy Spirit has bound us to the testimony of the first witnesses as well as more recent ones, to be tested in the messy crosswinds of everyday life.

To be a chemist, a physicist, a musician, or an attorney, a newcomer to that discipline has to trust other people. The novice never starts from scratch. The novice learns a tradition from current practitioners and a whole chain of predecessors. A certain amount of trust is necessary. Not gullibility, but trust. In very nearly the same way, to be a Christian involves a certain humility: the humility of paying attention to the tradition handed on by practitioners of the faith down to our own generation.

A Canadian theologian was teaching at a denominational conference center. He was asked to serve on a committee planning a worship service. The committee was struggling with how to put the service together. The theologian suggested, "We could say the Nicene Creed." Dead silence. After a long pause, someone said, "Well, maybe we could have people stand up for the parts they agree with and sit down for the parts they don't agree with." Can you imagine the bobbing up and down? As though the worshiping assembly should be required to vote, instantly and without forewarning, line by line, on the faith of the church?

At Christmastime, one is likely to hear a reading about angels appearing to the shepherds, and how the shepherds went to the manger to find Mary and Joseph and the baby. The shepherds reported to the new parents what they had heard from the angelic chorus. Luke tells us, "But Mary treasured all these words and pondered them in her heart" (Luke 2:19).

What Does "Ponder" Mean?

"Pondering" has to do with reflecting—respectfully reflecting over a period of time, and reflecting deeply, first from one angle, then from another; sometimes vigorously, sometimes quietly; sometimes letting doubt take the lead, sometimes doubting our doubts; sometimes leaning on intuition, sometimes following where the heart directs. And this, I think, is how we are to learn the faith of the church from all who have gone before us, including from saints we know personally, some we know only by reputation, and from a long line of practitioners of the faith all the way back to Thomas and to Matthew, Mark, Luke, and John. It's not a matter of deciding, today or tomorrow, or by some arbitrary deadline, that at last we fully understand and either believe or don't. Rather, to ponder is a lifelong commitment to revisiting the affirmations of the gospel over and over again, every time bringing with us every new experience, every new insight, every new question, with hands open, ready to receive whatever God may give us. And what God gives us today may be different from what was given a decade ago or may be given a decade hence.

What God will give is wrapped in a *magnum mysterium*—a monumental mystery. "Mystery" is not like a Rubik's cube that we can figure out if we stick with it long enough. "Mystery" is not a problem to be solved, a puzzle to be explained. "Mystery" is something profoundly true—yet too big, too deep, ever to be entirely within our grasp. "Mystery" is to be pondered, with reverence, all our lives long. "Mystery"—treasured—as Mary treasured the puzzling words of the shepherds—mystery takes us by the hand and leads us to places always new, ever challenging. Mystery leads us to the God become manifest in the risen Christ, who will not send us away empty.

I don't know exactly what God will give you in this lifelong process of pondering should you persevere in it. But I feel confident about this: God will give you something. You won't go away with nothing. We won't see the nail prints in Jesus' hands, or the wound in his side, with our own eyes. We won't reach out and touch his resurrection body. But we shall nevertheless "see" if we're willing to treasure and revisit what must always remain a mystery.

"Lord, I believe; help my unbelief."

A Preacher's Reflections: Ascension

"*We trust him to overcome every power that can hurt or divide us,*" we pray in the Canadian Presbyterian *anamnesis*.

What do we make of Jesus "ascending" to heaven? Is heaven really "up"? If it is, then where are we starting from? "Up" from Nashville or Pittsburgh? Or "up" from Sydney or Melbourne?

The Ascension of the Lord is not about "up" or "down." It's not about whether heaven is up in reference to the northern or the southern hemisphere. It's not even about whether heaven can be said to be a locatable place at all. When the Bible tells the story of Jesus ascending into heaven, it's resorting to what John Calvin called "baby talk." After his resurrection, Jesus took leave of his disciples and ascended into heaven, to sit at the right hand of the Father. Wait a minute. Sitting? Does God sit? Or stand? And does God have hands? I don't think so. It's baby talk. Picture language. And what it means is that Jesus Christ, having been executed in disgrace and raised in glory, has been lifted above all other authorities, and revealed to be Lord of all. "I have heard of your faith in the Lord Jesus," the apostle wrote to the church at Ephesus (Eph 1:15).

"Lord Jesus," a familiar phrase to people who go to church. It is easy enough to say, when we need to. If we were to take it seriously, we would probably choke on it. Because to go so far as to declare that "Jesus is Lord" puts us on record as saying that no one else is. No one else is Lord. There are, of course, many lawful authorities in this world and many enviable role models. They are worthy of our respect, for the most part. But, if Jesus is Lord, then nobody else can be. That's why the only Christians in North Korea are underground, in both senses of that word. There used to be many churches in Pyongyang. Now, all the believers are, indeed, beneath the ground. Because Kim Jong-Un and his team know what it means to call

Jesus "Lord," even if we are not too sure. If Jesus is Lord, then the "Supreme Leader" is not Lord. Nor is any other, whatever their politics.

To say that Jesus is Lord is a dangerous thing, and a radical act. The word "radical," by the way, doesn't mean "extreme." It comes from a Latin word, *radix*, which means "root." In other words, to take a radical position is to take a position that begins all the way down at the roots. It's foundational, it's basic, everything else leads from that. To affirm Jesus as Lord is to say that Jesus is our "true north," so to speak. It's a commitment to set our internal compasses in relation to him. It's by him that we get our bearings and steer our little ships. It's by him that we orient ourselves in the world.

People reorient themselves physically and spatially when they move from one place to another, from the prairies to the mountains, for example. But there are other ways of reorienting ourselves, and most of us know a little bit about that. We reorient ourselves from one world to another when we become a parent. And we reorient ourselves from one universe to another when we get sick. And we recalculate our position in the world when we move from employee to employer, or from employed to unemployed. "Recalculating," as the annoying voice on the GPS used to say when we had made an unexpected departure from the specified route. We recalculate, reorient ourselves from the roots on up when we move from rags to riches, or from riches to rags. When we affirm Jesus as Lord, it calls for us to recalculate our orientation in the world, to reset our compasses.

The apostle wrote to the church in Ephesus, "I have heard of your faith in the Lord Jesus," and then he expresses his appreciation for the people there and promises to pray for them. The apostle tells them what he's going to pray for. He's going to pray that God would give them "a spirit of wisdom and revelation as you come to know him [Christ]" (Eph 1:17). That's an interesting phrase, I think. The apostle wants wisdom for them, and revelation—but note the phrase, "as you come to know him—[Christ]." It's a process, then, isn't it? Not all accomplished at once. The members of the little church already have "faith in the Lord Jesus" and love for each other. But they're still coming to know him.

Sounds good. And how is that going to happen? Another curious phrase: they're going to come to know Christ with "the eyes of their hearts enlightened" (1:18). Wait just a minute! The heart has no optical nerve, does it? And its function is to pump, isn't it? But you don't really need an explanation, do you, that the apostle is speaking metaphorically? He is coining a figure of speech. The metaphor speaks for itself, and I won't insult you by trying to explain it. We come to know the Lord Jesus with the eyes of the heart. In the same way, the Scripture is speaking metaphorically when it pictures Jesus ascending to heaven. The three-dimensional image of ascension, of rising up, of elevation, signals that Jesus is Lord—in other words, above everything that is—sovereign. We look to him to clarify what matters most.

In the service of baptism, and again at Confirmation, the pastor asks, on behalf of the whole church, that those involved both affirm their faith that Jesus is Lord, and renounce any other claimants. It goes something like this: "Do you renounce all evil, and powers in the world which defy God's righteousness and love?"

But what are we renouncing? Is it just monstrous evil, like the Armenian and Rwandan genocides? Like the holocaust? Well, of course, that's a part of it. But it's easy to renounce those sorts of evil, since it's clear how horrible they are, and ordinarily they tend to be comparatively far away from us. But there's evil nearer at hand. Evil is even more than my doing something cruel, mean, nasty—or you doing something unlawful. Evil is manifest in and among well-meaning and well-behaved people. Evil manifests itself in complex systems that seduce us and co-opt us and often benefit us even when we don't even see them. When the way things are done nearly guarantees that some voices will be heard and others won't be. When whoever has the biggest bucks rules. When it turns out that the rules of the game virtually guarantee that the same winners will keep winning, and winning, and winning—and the same losers keep losing, and losing, and keep on losing even when they have nothing left any more to lose.

When we renounce evil and its powers in the world, we're saying what we have discerned with the eyes of our hearts: that Jesus is Lord, and that Jesus is *our* Lord; and that we're willing, if need be, to take some losses for the sake of what's true, and right, and good. Jesus is Lord, and Jesus is our Lord, and so we're prepared to take a good look at how things actually work in this world—not just how they're supposed to work according to what we memorized in order to pass the high school civics quiz. And having taken a good look, we who belong to the Lord Jesus are called to stand by the designated losers even if it means taking some hits ourselves. Of course, we are actually too human not to feel threatened by the powers. We are too frightened. There's too much at stake. There are too many intimidating ways to persuade us to back down. Except that God has power, too. This is what it looks like: "God put this power to work in Christ when he raised him from the dead and seated him at his right hand in the heavenly places, far above all rule and authority and power and dominion, and above every name that is named, not only in this age but also in the age to come" (1:20, 21). "*We trust him to overcome every power that can hurt or divide us.*"

A Preacher's Reflections: "Universal Restoration"

The Presbyterian Church of Canada's *anamnesis* gives serious attention to the promise of the *parousia*. "When he comes in glory we will celebrate victory with him." The one who will come in glory is Jesus, who healed the sick, sat down for meals with sinners, lifted up the poor, chased away personal storms to restore balance and return folks to their right minds. In Jesus, those with eyes to see and ears to hear have already witnessed God's disposition towards us. And God's disposition is more than generous. That's the reason the so-called "second coming" has always been about good news, not bad news. About redemption, not damnation. About a new creation, a new heaven and a new earth. About "universal restoration," as Peter calls it in his sermon (Acts 3:21). About the universe healed and repaired, balance restored, God showing God's hand openly, publicly, unmistakably, for every creature to see without ambiguity. There will be a moment when the Lordship of Jesus, already discernible with the eyes of faith, will become apparent to the whole creation. That is what "second coming" is all about. If you missed it when it came in humility the first time, you won't miss it the second time, when he comes in glory.

The church prays every time we gather: "Your kingdom come." Jesus promises that God's eternal reign is going to come. That God is going to have the last word. And that last word is about a redemption that reaches further than we may have imagined.

On that day, Jesus says, "Then two will be in the field; one will be taken and one will be left. Two women will be grinding meal together; one will be taken and one will be left" (Matt 24:40–41). What does that mean? It may mean that things will be, in that moment, as they are right now and always have been; one believes, while another does not. One responds in faith and joy; another, equally intelligent, no less moral, every bit as "decent" a human being, responds with indifference, or bewilderment. There is a certain mystery here, akin to the parable of the sower (Matt 13:24–30). Decent people, exposed to the same gospel, respond to it quite differently. One hears, and finds her inner world transformed. Another hears the same word, and, skeptical, disdainful, or indifferent, shrugs it off. It's not a simple case of good people believing and bad people not. The mysterious difference inspires all sorts of unhealthy speculation, but we had just as well acknowledge the mystery and leave it alone.

For whatever reason, at the last day of ordinary history, as in all the other days, one hears and believes; another keeps on grinding corn or harvesting wheat. One looks up to see salvation at hand; another keeps on vacuuming, or trying to get a bug out of a computer program. Why so? All Jesus tells us is that on the day of the *parousia*, people will still be people, with their various ways of dealing.

Does that mean that there is no hope for the ones who, like the faithful, come face to face with the One who brings the reign of God, but nevertheless go right on with their shopping? Once we pose that question, we find ourselves on shaky ground. It is fruitless to speculate about other people. While we trust the incredible generosity of a gracious God, our first obligation is to tend to our own response. "Keep awake therefore, for you do not know on what day your Lord is coming . . . Therefore you also must be ready, for the Son of Man is coming at an unexpected hour" (Matt 24:44).

Bear in mind that Jesus was speaking to his disciples at a time when the axe was about to fall on him and, perhaps indirectly, on them. "When Jesus had finished saying all these things, he said to his disciples, 'You know that after two days the Passover is coming, and the Son of Man will be handed over to be crucified'" (Matt 26:1–2).

Jesus and the disciples were approaching a moment of crisis, involving the temple police, a rigged trial, and a cross. His words projecting another sort of crisis on another day were meant to comfort them. Not only would God be present in every extreme moment, but all human history is ultimately in God's hands. Jesus invited his disciples to imagine what would be the outermost moments of ordinary time, and still be, at the very same time, the dawn of God's *basileia*. And what would they discover should they experience that day of extremes? They would find, on what will be both last day and first day, a landscape in which the central figure will be the one who had had no place to lay his head. He who ate with sinners and lifted up the poor and the sick will be recognized as the One who will make "all things new" (Rev 21:5).

Jesus offered his disciples a vision of this landscape of extremes both to strengthen them to face the crisis that was immediately at hand, and to reassure them. While it is true that this vision has a terrifying dimension to it, Jesus wanted his disciples to know that there will be a sharp awakening as the era of ordinary time gives way to the *basileia*. Those who had misunderstood him and his disciples and those who had misrepresented him and treated him contemptibly will, on that day, face the truth. And the truth is a person: Jesus Christ.

That last day/first day, the *parousia*, will be the day when the last sword is beaten into a plowshare, and the last spear turned into a pruning hook. It will be the day on which the crooked will be made straight, and no Super PAC political image–makers can make it crooked again. Fearful it will be, yes; awesome, of course. But in that hour we shall all meet that One who healed those with chronic diseases and raised the dead. In that moment, the One who loves extravagantly and urges forgiveness even for those who crucify him is coming to meet us. "Then Jesus said, Father, forgive them; for they do not know what they are doing" (Luke 23:34a).

Be reminded that what Jesus is doing in his apocalyptic narrative is to describe the undescribable with the help of a story, a narrative that highlights the drama of God's ultimate confrontation with the powers and principalities.

> For our struggle is not against enemies of blood and flesh, but against the rulers, against the authorities, against the cosmic powers of this present darkness, against the spiritual forces of evil in the heavenly places. Therefore take up the whole armor of God, so that you may be able to withstand on that evil day, and having done everything, to stand firm. (Eph 6:12–13)

The imperative—"stand firm"—is clear enough. Beyond that, we may dare to hope that even those who cannot or will not "stand firm," or even know what it means, will somehow be embraced by the generous God whose heart is revealed in Jesus Christ. The apostle Paul seems to cherish the same hope. "For God has imprisoned all in disobedience so that he may be merciful to all" (Rom 11:32).

All of this and more is suggested in a single sentence of the *anamnesis*: "*He is still the friend of sinners. We trust him to overcome every power that can hurt or divide us, and believe that when he comes in glory we will celebrate victory with him.*"

A Preacher's Reflections: The Mystery of Faith

The words of institution normally follow as the concluding words of the *anamnesis*. Of course, while the Last Supper was the occasion when Jesus invited the disciples to "remember" him in this meal, the Lord's Supper is not meant to be a replay of his last meal. Another meal, not long after the one that preceded Jesus' death, may be the first *Lord's* Supper.

On the very first Easter, at least a couple of people in the circle of those who had gathered around Jesus had lost faith. Or were at risk of losing it. They were on the road, headed for Emmaus, a village about seven miles from Jerusalem. They were reeling from what they knew and what they didn't know. Jesus was dead, and not dead from high cholesterol or emphysema, but dead in a way that marked him as cursed. They could read it right there, in Deut 21:23: "For anyone hung on a tree is under God's curse."

That's not the way it was supposed to have worked out—at least in their minds. The coming of Christ, the Messiah, the anointed one was meant to be all about winning big. Triumph, victory, all glory all the time. Not crosses. Oh, sure, they'd heard a rumor that "some women" of their group had gone to the tomb and "seen a vision of angels who said that he was alive" (Luke 24:23). Crazy talk. Grief can do that sort of thing to you. So the two travelers plodded on, more bewildered with every step. They'd been filled with the sense that, in Jesus' company, they'd been on the very edge of something really, really big. That God was in it. So what now? How to make sense of it?

A stranger joined the two travelers. We know who the stranger was, but "Their eyes were kept from recognizing him," Luke says. The stranger was curious about their animated conversation. "What are you discussing with each other?" (24:16–17). They brought him up to speed, telling how the authorities had caused Jesus to be crucified. "But we had hoped"—*had* hoped; note the past-participle here—"that he was the one to redeem Israel" (24:21). Game over, it seemed.

The stranger began sorting through familiar Scripture, connecting the dots, putting the puzzle together, slowly bringing the whole picture into focus. "Was it not necessary," he asked, "that the Messiah should suffer these things and then enter into his glory?" (24:26).

Of course, we don't have a record of exactly how this traveling Bible study might have proceeded. Here's my guess. My guess is that the two disillusioned disciples were disturbed by that curse in Deuteronomy: "For anyone hung on a tree is under God's curse." Maybe the stranger explained that the one place the Messiah was surely meant to be was right there on the cursed tree, among all those who had been cursed, damned, written off, kicked out, ruined. The later church put it like this, as we know it in the Apostles' Creed: "He descended to the dead." Or, more vividly, "He descended into hell." That descent to be with the cursed ones was no accident. It was his calling, his mission, his purpose.

> For this is the reason the gospel was proclaimed even to the dead, so that, though they had been judged in the flesh as everyone is judged, they might live in the spirit as God does. (1 Pet 4:6)

Where the cursed are, there is the Christ. Where there is anyone in hell, there is the Christ. Where the outcast, the unclean, the shunned are, there is the Christ. So, maybe they talked about Deuteronomy. Or maybe the stranger quoted the prophet Isaiah: "He poured out himself to death, and was numbered with the transgressors; yet he bore the sin of many, and made intercession for the transgressors" (Isa 53:12). God's suffering Servant intercedes for "the transgressors," would you believe—and anyone in any kind of transgressors' hell. "Then beginning with Moses and all the prophets, he interpreted to them the things about himself in all the scriptures" (Luke 24:27).

There's a sense in which Jesus' voice is always the voice of a stranger, always mediated through the voice of another—in this instance, perhaps the voice mediated by Luke's Gospel. The authoritative voice one may learn to discern in Scripture is often drowned out by the sheer abundance and volume of other voices. But it hasn't gone silent. It may be manifest in the voice of one who preaches, believe it or not—or a voice hidden in the words of a scholar or even a novelist or poet, or a voice set to music, or speaking in the voice of a child or a stranger. No matter the medium, his voice always does the same thing: clears some things up; unsettles others. If you pay attention, Jesus' voice, interpreting Scripture, wakes you up.

The travelers reached their destination, but they were so absorbed in their discussion that they wanted to keep the conversation going. They invited the stranger to join them for the evening meal. Here's what happened, as Luke tells it: "When he was at table with them, he took bread, blessed and broke it, and gave it to them" (24:30). The Gospel writer intends the sequence of verbs to be noticed: The traveling companion *took*, *blessed*, *broke*, and *gave* bread. The same verbs in the same sequence occur in the account of the Last Supper, and in the stories of the feeding of the multitudes, and now, in this post-Resurrection meal. It's not an accident.

Something is going on here. What was it? "Then their eyes were opened, and they recognized him" (24:31).

First, he had cracked the Scriptures open, fitted the broken pieces of the story together, and they'd been intrigued, then absorbed and heartened by what he had shown them. And in the process, their profound sadness had begun to lift. If the stranger could be believed, God had in fact been in it all along, and was still in it, cross and all. And then came the meal. It was an experience of quite a different order from the discussion on the road. Something different from—and more than—just getting the picture. Eyes opened! Recognition!

One can have perfect twenty-twenty vision and fail to see what really matters. Sometimes it seems as though it takes a miracle to see all the way to the heart of things. And that, I guess, is what Luke says happened here. This was the first *Lord's Supper*, and it was not a melancholy replay of a departure, a last meal, but it was a joyful meal, the first meal anticipating a new era. The disciples found themselves on the threshold of the reign of God, and they saw with new eyes the companion who had been with them all along. In his presence, they could see all the way to how everything—everything—was going to turn out. What they saw in that meal, in the breaking of the bread, was an insight into the very heart of things. What people of faith glimpse right now, by faith, will one day be universally known. Millennia may come and go. Churches may be built and fall into ruin; the nations, sometimes at least respectful of this faith, on the one hand, sometimes marked by indifference or even contempt on the other. The triune God honored here, ignored there. Ages will pass, and the One who has always been here, traveling with us, will be revealed—not just to people of faith, but to one and all. "Then the eyes of the blind shall be opened . . . [and] "the glory of the Lord shall be revealed, and all people shall see it together," just as the prophet had said (Isa 35:5).

On the way to Emmaus, after the eye-opening vision at the table, the stranger "vanished from their sight." The two travelers jumped up from the table, hurried back to Jerusalem, found the disheartened eleven, and managed to stammer out their story: how their hearts had burned within them as he had interpreted Scripture on the road, and how "he had been made known to them in the breaking of the bread" (24:35). From then on, and for generations following, whenever Christians met, every Lord's Day—not just quarterly, not just once a month, but every Lord's Day—they listened for the voice of the Lord in Scripture, and shared a meal at which the crucified and risen Christ was host, as well as becoming the manna provided in our every wilderness. Every Sunday, an encounter with Christ in Scripture is paired with an encounter with Christ in the Eucharist, both of them reinforcing and strengthening his presence sacramentally. Word, preparing us to identify Christ in the sacrament; and sacrament, leading us to the Christ who nourishes us with the word.

In our own Emmaus journeys, accompanied by One whose voice can help us put the pieces together; and in the common meal in which we discern his identity and take comfort in his presence, our eyes may be opened enough to see all the way to the heart of things. This is the hope that sustains and animates the church of Christ. This is the true story of the world, even when steeples are falling: that in a day of God's own choosing, "the glory of the Lord shall be revealed" (Isa 40:5). *"This is the mystery of faith!"*

And the response, sung or said:
Christ has died!
Christ is risen!
Christ will come again!

7

Preaching the Holy Spirit and the Messianic Banquet

The Communion of the Holy Spirit . . .

IN THE EUCHARISTIC LITURGIES of the Orthodox churches of the east, invocation of the Holy Spirit is essential. For John Calvin, whose understanding of the Eucharist may have been influenced by Chrysostom, the Holy Spirit was central to sacramental theology, even though that did not become evident in his liturgy. The newer eucharistic prayers, introduced ecumenically, have been influenced by the eastern models.

The third movement of the Great Thanksgiving is called by its classical Greek name, *epiclesis*. The *epiclesis* is a prayer for the blessing of the Holy Spirit, the third person of the Trinity, who is at work in us, with us, and among us, and at work in the world for those with eyes to discern. Without the Holy Spirit, there is no sacrament. The Spirit enables *presence*. Christ present to us and us to Christ; and each of us present to each other. Bread and wine and the actions that center around them in the assembled congregation become the physical means that embody the promise of presence. One version of the *epiclesis* is this one for Trinity Sunday from the PCUSA *Book of Common Worship*.

> Gracious God, pour out your Holy Spirit upon us and upon these your gifts of bread and wine, that the bread we break and the cup we bless may be the communion of the body and blood of Christ. By your Spirit make us one with Christ that we may be one with all who share this feast, united in ministry in every place. As this

bread is Christ's body for us, send us out to be the body of Christ in the world. Keep us faithful in your service until Christ comes in final victory and we shall feast with all your saints in the joy of your eternal realm.[1]

Gracious God, pour out your Holy Spirit upon us and upon these your gifts of bread and wine, that the bread we break and the cup we bless may be the communion of the body and blood of Christ.

In Protestant churches, one may see on many altars or Communion tables the words, "Do this in remembrance of me." These words are biblical, of course, and not unimportant. It was striking, then, to hear a sacramental theologian suggest that the words that appear on the altar/table might rather be "Holy, Holy, Holy." Why?

It may be because many Protestants are inclined to think of the Lord's Supper as intended to remind us of something we are in danger of forgetting: Jesus' death on the cross. So the words, like the bread and wine, are presumably meant to stir the memory, turn our thoughts back, far back, to the distant past, when our Savior became the target of the rage of the religious authorities, the secular hierarchy, and a significant number of the public, who cried, "Crucify him!" (Mark 15:13).

The interpretation of the sacrament as a kind of memorial, a sort of funeral for a dead Jesus, has influenced many generations to imagine that the tone of the Eucharist is meant to be penitential, regretful, a monument to a terrible grief that we are all too likely to forget. "Remember," then, has been taken as an imperative directed toward us, the forgetful congregation.

Both before and after the Reformation, Catholics and Protestants tended to agree on this one thing—that the sacrament was intended, as at least one of its elements, to make us feel sorry. That penitential quality has faded in recent decades, partly because of the actions of the Second Vatican Council and subsequent Protestant reforms, but the sense that the sacrament was meant to direct our gaze back to a sad moment in time continues to exert considerable influence. That is so in spite of the fact that the new denominational service books provide texts that do not intend to lead us to look only at the past, but also to accent the sacramental present, and, just as significantly, look to the future. When the newer texts are not used, or the congregation encounters them only occasionally and without any orientation to them, the people are often left to interpret the sacrament on their

1. Presbyterian Church in Canada, *Book of Common Worship*, 357.

own, informed in part by what are often somber musical accompaniments that reinforce the tone familiar from the past. The word that resonates most decisively is the word "remembrance," as though remembering is only about a retrospective view.

It is fitting to remember and be reminded to remember, but there may be more to remembering than only recalling an event in the past. In the Bible, we find examples of human beings urging *God* to remember. Not that the holy One is likely to forget something important or need a reminder.

> There are many Old Testament precedents in which an appeal is made for God to remember. For example, when Israel in the wilderness had become dismayed at Moses' long absence and had fashioned the golden calf, Moses responded to God's subsequent wrath. Moses pleaded for the people, reminding God of God's own covenant . . . "Remember [Hebrew, *zkr*] Abraham, Isaac, and Israel, your servants, how you swore to them, 'I will multiply your descendants like the stars of heaven, and all this land that I have promised I will give to your descendants, and they shall inherit it forever'" (Exod 32:13).[2]

The psalmist also pleaded with God, "Remember [*zkr*] your congregation, which you acquired long ago, which you redeemed to be the tribe of your heritage" (Ps 74:2). The rainbow in the heavens after the great flood was a sign of a divine promise. "When the bow is in the clouds I [YHWH] will see it and remember [*zkr*] the everlasting covenant between God and every living creature of all flesh that is on the earth" (Gen 9:16).

"Jesus' death is not just a past event; it plays a role in God's eternal purpose. The praying church holds it up for *God's* 'remembrance' as an earnest plea that God's purpose may be realized now."[3] "Do this in remembrance of me" is not merely a reminder to Christ's disciples in every age, but it is also a way of calling upon God to follow through on the promises implicit in Jesus' death, resurrection, ascension, and promise to come again. In other words, it is a prayer to God for the realization of the promised reign of Christ. Note the change in direction: we look backward in order to look forward. The heart of the gospel, the Christian hope framed on a large screen, the big picture, if you will, is of a moment when God will realize the promise, "See, I am making all things new" (Rev 21:5). Peter's sermon in Solomon's Portico testifies to "Jesus, who must remain in heaven until the

---

2. Byars, *Sacraments*, 192.
3. Byars, *Sacraments*, 194.

time of universal restoration that God announced long ago through the prophets" (Acts 3:21).

In the typical use of "remembrance" we are not well prepared to notice the nuance in the word. That may inadvertently narrow our perspective, as it has for many generations. To see the altar/table in a way that may enable remembering forward as well as backward, it may be helpful, should we choose to adorn it with any words at all, to choose these: "Holy, Holy, Holy." And those words are even more appropriate when we are reminded that, in addition to looking backward in order to look forward, at the altar/table we find ourselves at a meeting place. In other words, the host of the meal becomes sacramentally present to us, by the Spirit, in our assembly. Holy! Holy! Holy!

It is in hope of this "presence" that we turn to the third person of the Holy Trinity, praying to God for the Holy Spirit to *"pour out your Holy Spirit upon us and upon these your gifts of bread and wine."* And what is it that we are expecting when we pray for the outpouring of the Holy Spirit? Are we praying that the physical substances of bread and wine will be metaphysically changed, so that in some way they become Christ's literal flesh and blood? The churches of the Reformation have been led to perceive "real presence" differently. It is true that at the Last Supper, Jesus said, "This is my body, which is given for you" (Luke 22:19), and "This cup that is poured out for you is the new covenant in my blood" (22:20). These words ought to be read alongside Jesus' words in the Gospel of John, where he recalls God's gift of manna in the wilderness, and tells his audience that "it was not Moses who gave you the bread from heaven, but it is my Father who gives you the true bread from heaven" (John 6:32). Those listening "said to him, 'Sir, give us this bread always'" (6:34), whereupon "Jesus said to them, '*I am* the bread of life'" (6:35, italics by the author).

The words "I am" are not merely utilitarian. They are used intentionally for the purpose of calling to mind Moses' experience with the bush that was burning, but not consumed. God spoke to Moses from the burning bush, but Moses insisted on knowing God's name, in case the people whom Moses had been called to lead should require some identification. God's response was, "I AM WHO I AM" (Exod 3:14), and added, "Thus you shall say to the Israelites, 'I AM has sent me to you.'" (3:15).

When Jesus says, "I am," whether in the synoptic Gospels or in John, we should be alert to the double meaning. It is both grammatically appropriate and used as an intentional signal to identify Jesus with the One who spoke to Moses in the burning bush. The intentionality behind this usage is particularly evident in John, where Jesus is said to have made "I am" statements several times:

"I am the light of the world." (9:5)

"I am the gate" (10:7)

"I am the good shepherd" (10:11)

"I am the resurrection and the life" (11:25)

"I am the way, the truth, and the life" (14:6)

When Jesus said, "I am the bread of life" (which we might quite accurately print as "I AM the bread of life"), should we understand him to be saying that, with prayer, his literal flesh is recreated and served at the table? It is rather more likely that the Gospel writers understood him to be saying that in some sense he is to us what the manna from heaven was to the people of Israel. In other words, he is our sustenance, he is our food, our nourishment, in "wilderness times"—unsettled times, uncertain times, times of desperation as well as ordinary times. He is, borrowing the words of the psalmist, "bread to strengthen the human heart," and "wine to gladden the human heart" (Ps 104:15).

In a sense that can be understood intuitively by those who press on in faith, the person of Jesus is truly our bread and our wine. No metaphysical theories are required for this to be true. He sustains us, and gladdens our hearts. When he tells his disciples at the Last Supper that the bread he has broken is his body, and the cup poured out is his blood, the various "I AM" statements come to mind. What is he offering to those who are his disciples? He is offering himself a human being who is both flesh and blood like us while he is at the same time the eternal One, indeed, the great I AM. He is fully present, sacramentally, which is to say, in a fashion that makes use of words, actions, even taste, all meant to unfold to heart and mind what would otherwise not be visible, tangible, or comprehensible. Christ becomes both our guest and our host, as well as our nourishment.

How can such a thing be? Especially since there is so much distance in time, and so much history has elapsed since he made this promise to those gathered with him in an upper room? It happens by means of the third "person" of the Trinity: the Holy Spirit. We may be confident that the promise will be kept, whether we are paying attention or whether we are distracted by the child who accompanies us to the altar/table or by our own

Preaching the Holy Spirit and the Messianic Banquet

preoccupation; whether we register his presence emotionally or intellectually, or neither one. The gift is a promise and it is reliable. Jesus gives us not some piece of himself, but the whole of himself: our food and drink as we navigate this life.

The Holy Spirit enables us to receive the promise represented not in the bread and wine alone, but in the whole action of the sacrament: *taking* the bread, thankfully *blessing* it, *breaking* it, and *giving* it, all in the context of an assembly of the baptized. Thanking and blessing includes, in the *epiclesis*, the prayer *that the bread we break and the cup we bless may be the communion of the body and blood of Christ.*

Holy! Holy! Holy!

In other words, our prayer is that the Spirit may kindle our imaginations so as to enable us to perceive the gift given and be strengthened by it, along with those who share the meal with us, near and far, *that we may be one with all who share this feast, united in ministry in every place.* The apostle Paul wrote, "For all who eat and drink without discerning the body, eat and drink judgment against themselves" (1 Cor 11:29). To "discern the body" is not about agreeing on a theory about what may happen to the bread and wine, but to be able to recognize the assorted communicants who gather at the altar/table to be members of the body of Christ, as unlikely as it may seem from casual appearances. Here the Spirit enables us to see beyond superficialities, and strengthens us to accept the covenantal responsibility that we share with these same persons along with others not personally known to us, making us one with all who share the feast. Together we are part of Christ's church. And Christ's church, like Israel, serves as a kind of shared priesthood, with a priestly vocation that might be described as a calling to be intercessors and advocates (Exod 19:6; Isa 61:6; 1 Pet 2:9; Rev 1:6; 5:10). That apostolic vocation is acknowledged as we pray for the Spirit to lead us to where God is sending us, as expressed in the prayer: *"As this bread is Christ's body for us, send us out to be the body of Christ in the world."*

A Preacher's Reflections: When Christ comes . . .

Israelis have not been successful in helping Palestinians comprehend the trauma of the gas chambers and the mass graves that drove them out of Europe. And Palestinians have not been successful at helping Israelis perceive their trauma as a colonized people, cast out of ancestral lands and homes since 1948. The scripts that we play in our own heads drown out the voices of the other.

We have a problem here, and it's not a new one but a very old one. This problem is not going to be solved by language lessons or by Google's electronic translation program. The problem here is not about the fact that the French and the Serbs have different words for things; it's not about grammar or syntax or even accents. We have a problem here, and it runs deeper than that. It's a soul-sickness problem that manifests as a language problem. How can I explain myself to you when I don't understand myself? From childhood, we learn how to use words to mislead, confuse, and disarm. We are offended and indignant and resentful of meanings no one intended. I see your mouth moving but I'm not listening, and you register my voice, but are busy rehearsing your rebuttal. We both speak and hear defensively.

We've got a problem here. Anybody who lives with anybody else, or works with other people, already knows that. Maybe we could solve the problem if we just *explained* ourselves more clearly. Do you think? Maybe if we just chose our words more carefully? A history teacher complains that the students in her course normally leave the class with exactly the same prejudices they brought into it. Having read the books and heard the lectures, they have learned better arguments to support opinions rooted in the gender, class, racial, family, and social certainties they brought to class with them. Every parent or child knows that you can explain your point of view eloquently, to no avail. There's something deeper at work here than can be solved by explaining ourselves more clearly. It is a soul-sick problem.

The problem is not new. The apostles, gathered in Jerusalem on the Jewish feast of Pentecost, summoned their courage to speak in public for the first time after Jesus' ascension. The message is, "The one who was crucified has been vindicated. He is Lord of all." What are the passing crowds likely to hear? All they are likely to hear is that this peculiar person, this Nazarene the apostles are proclaiming, had been crucified. Crucified! The book of Deuteronomy says that anybody who's crucified is cursed (Deut 21:23). And to witness that grotesque sight, the crosses of crucified criminals lining the road—and to hear the tortured cries and the scornful jeering of passers-by—was to know that it was so. Those who were crucified were damned. The apostles spoke of "glory." Their audience would have heard "godforsaken."

But—miracle of miracles—the twisted speech, the typically human distortions of perception were healed for that Pentecost moment. What's out of reach for human beings is not out of reach for the Holy Spirit. Pentecost was a Jewish festival day. The city was filled with people from all over the Mediterranean basin. They were all Jews, but they spoke the languages they had grown up with back home. The apostles dared a little street preaching. They spoke in their native Galilean accents, a dialect of the Aramaic language. They may as well have been speaking Eskimo. But—and here's the miracle—Scripture says that the apostles "were filled with the Holy Spirit and began to speak in other languages, as the Spirit gave them ability" (Acts 2:4).

Now, this seems pretty far-fetched, doesn't it? Something has happened—something remarkable—something beyond the capacity of a journalist to comprehend, much less describe. And Luke, who recorded the story, has had to find a way to tell it.

You and I can't really get behind the biblical text. We can't peel it away to uncover what a neutral observer might have seen, whether to approve the story or scoff at it. All we have is the story as Luke crafted it—but the story is enough, because it tells us that God made connections where no connections might have been expected. It's as astonishing as though Kamala Harris had made a speech about inclusiveness, and Tucker Carlson gave a thumbs-up and invited her for an interview on the Fox network.

The apostles proclaimed to the motley crowd that a crucified man was the Messiah; that God had vindicated him by raising him from the bonds of death; that he was *Lord of all*! And the crowd, the suspicious crowd, the skeptical crowd, the crowd that knew their Bible and had quite different expectations—this crowd of people who couldn't order a pizza in a Jerusalem restaurant because they didn't know a word of the local language—this resistant audience heard the proclamation that a crucified man was Lord of all, and they cried out, "Amen!" "We hear you! Right on! Amen!"

Luke is telling us about a miracle that has two parts: the first part is a miracle of speaking: the apostles "began to speak in other languages, as the Spirit gave them ability" (2:4). But the second part is a miracle of hearing. "Each one heard them speaking in the native language of each" (2:6). God is at work here, doing something that mortals cannot do, even with the best of intentions. God brings about a breakthrough of enormous proportions—one that's about more than separate languages. Language barriers serve to symbolize the soul-sickness that turns human communication into a minefield.

Out of this miracle of comprehension, the Holy Spirit, the blessed Spirit, the gracious Spirit of God called out to a diverse crowd of strangers and gathered the church. By some continuing miracle, the Spirit still manages to speak through the church, in spite of our linguistic incapacities and our complacency and our obsession with the trivial. The Spirit uses even our agonizing wordiness. And, believe it or not, in spite of the fact that we who deliver the message so frequently disappoint, the miracle still happens: some folks hear it, deeply and truly.

One wonders if, in this time when there is an excess of words assaulting us twenty-four-seven, whether maybe it would be good to look more closely at the second half of the miracle: the miracle of hearing. Maybe the church can rediscover its usefulness in the world by majoring for a while in careful listening. It may be that what the world needs at the moment is a good listener; needs a people whose work it is to listen, on behalf of the other. It needs a broker to enable a mutual hearing, a mutual comprehension, even when words fail. Christians hearing Muslims, Palestinians hearing Israelis, Mayflower descendants hearing the immigrant who mows their lawns, the securely employed hearing the voice of the seven-year-old at the Salvation Army shelter: "Our family doesn't have a home any more; we just have a room."

The miracle of Pentecost is God's down payment on a far bigger project. Just as the New Testament stories about the healing of the blind, or the paralyzed, or the demon-possessed are about God's down payment on a far bigger project. And that project, God's project, is to fashion new heaven and a new earth, a new creation. One in which no one will be blind, in any sense of the word; and no one will be paralyzed, in any sense of the word. And no one will find themselves broken into pieces, whirled into confusion, unable to deal.

Peter, preaching on the day of Pentecost, recalled the prophet saying, "The sun shall be turned to darkness and the moon to blood, before the coming of the Lord's great and glorious day" (Acts 2:20). Sounds ominous, doesn't it? The natural world itself coming undone—undone in order that it might become something else—undone, for the moment, as it sucks in its breath waiting for "the Lord's great and glorious day."

The Spirit—not once, but more than once (you may have experienced it yourself!)—finds ways to break through the storms of sound that threaten to scramble all the words, including the word of God. The Spirit can subdue the static that distorts our hearing. Pentecost is a foretaste of what the

Lord's "great and glorious day" will be like everywhere and for everyone. It's a down payment on a repaired creation, a broken world refashioned. A day in which the resurrection of the Lord, and the Pentecost miracle, will make perfect sense—will be the obvious truth of things, clear as the full moon on a cloudless night. Perfect sense, because they clearly point to a transfigured creation that truly is to be—a transfigured creation, toward which God is working even now. It will be a day when the Spirit transforms your speech and mine; repairs your soul-sickness and mine: a "great and glorious day." "*When Christ comes in final victory.*"

A Preacher's Reflections: "We Shall Feast with All Your Saints in the Joy of Your Eternal Realm."

When my nephew was a teenager, his mother told me that she used to hear him singing in the shower. I suspect he had no idea that other people could hear him, but he would segue from some popular piece that everybody his age was listening to, and then sing lustily, "This is the feast of victory for our God! Alleluia! Alleluia! Alleluia!"[4] He had learned it, of course, worshiping with his parents at St. John Lutheran Church. I don't sing in the shower, but sometimes I hum to myself, and something that I might be tempted to hum might be that one: "This is the feast of victory for our God!"

It is rather surprising how many stories in the Bible—both testaments—have to do with meals. When the people of Israel had escaped from Egyptian bondage and were wandering in the wilderness, they became hungry, and began to remember fondly the food they had enjoyed when they were slaves. In response to their complaining, a gracious God gave them manna, provided for them every day in the wilderness places through which they were passing (Exod 16:4).

Jethro, Moses' father-in-law, celebrating what God had done "for Moses and for his people Israel" organized a banquet, and "all the elders of Israel" came to dine with him "in the presence of God" (18:1 and 12). In another instance, after God had given the law to the people through Moses, he, his brother Aaron, two of Aaron's sons, and seventy elders of Israel "went up, and they saw the God of Israel. They beheld God, and they ate and drank" (24:10, 11).

After the Babylonian captivity, when the people had reunited in Jerusalem, the scribe Ezra read the Torah to the assembled crowd, and they

---

4. Evangelical Lutheran Church in America, *Evangelical Lutheran Worship*, #165–66.

were deeply moved. Celebrating their renewal of the covenant, Nehemiah, the governor, said to them, "This day is holy to the LORD your God. . . .Go your way, eat the fat and drink sweet wine and send portions of them to those for whom nothing is prepared" (Neh 8:9–10).

Stories about both the prophet Elijah and his successor, Elisha, include stories about miraculous provisions of food (1 Kgs 17:7–16, and 2 Kgs 4:42–44), and these stories are echoed in all four Gospels in their accounts of Jesus' feedings of the multitudes. Exodus 12 describes the origins of the Passover meal, which has always had about it both an aspect of remembering backward to the exodus as well as looking forward to a future messianic redemption.

Eating and drinking, of course, is a practical need for all creatures, human and otherwise, but it has other purposes than the need for nourishment for the sake of biological survival. Meals shared with other people both represent and evoke a measure of intimacy. The child too young to walk, sitting at the table in a high chair, "knows" in some non-intellectual way what it is to belong, and to belong at this table and with these people. Some families are in a position to offer hospitality to persons who might be alone on a holiday. Their guests, one or several, could certainly manage to put together something edible with which to get by at home on their own, but even though those gathered may not always know one another, they feel connected at their host's table. Food and drink are life-giving for the spirit as well as the body. It is not surprising that, for some, at least sometimes, it may feel as though an ordinary meal has been graced with the presence of the divine.

On occasion, those at table know that the meal they are sharing is the last one they will have together. The new graduates will be scattering across the nation and even the world; they will meet new people and form new relationships. Among longtime friends, one is retiring and moving away; another is afflicted by an illness that she is not likely to survive until the next birthday or Christmas. Last meals, when it is known that they are last, or known in retrospect to have been last, are marked by a certain poignancy. Perhaps that is one reason that Jesus' last meal with his disciples has come to be more than just one more meal, or one more Passover. Recalling that last meal, disciples may have been reminded of earlier meals, including ones that Jesus shared with people who were outside the bounds of normal fraternization: tax collectors, and sinners. And the last meal probably laid a foundation for experiencing the meal that would follow the "last" one,

Preaching the Holy Spirit and the Messianic Banquet

where Jesus would become present to those he had surreptitiously joined on the road to Emmaus (Luke 24). In the upper room Jesus had said to the disciples, "I tell you, I will never again drink of this fruit of the vine until that day when I drink it new with you in my Father's kingdom" (Matt 26:29). The meal on the Emmaus Road was, perhaps, a down payment on that "kingdom" made manifest in the moment and as a promise of the victory to come when it shall be fully realized at last. "This is the feast of victory for our God!"

It is perhaps not surprising that the New Testament uses the image of a banquet to describe the coming reign of Christ, for which we pray in the prayer he taught his disciples. "The kingdom of heaven may be compared to a king who gave a wedding banquet for his son" (Matt 22:2). "Blessed is anyone who will eat bread in the kingdom of God!" (Luke 14:15), and "Blessed are those who are invited to the marriage supper of the Lamb" (Rev 19:9).

The guests at this meal "will come from east and west, from north and south, and will eat in the kingdom of God" (Luke 13:29), reminding those who know their Scriptures of the words of the psalmist.

> Let the redeemed of the LORD say so,
> > those he redeemed from trouble
> and gathered in from the lands,
> > from the east and from the west,
> > from the north and from the south. (Ps 107:2–3)

A homely way of picturing this great ingathering is as though it will resemble a great homecoming, with "dinner on the grounds," as they might say out in the country. Picture the cars parked along the road, close enough to the huge number of picnic tables all set up and ready to provide a place for you and whatever you may choose to share for the meal. License plates show that people have come from California, Florida, Nebraska, British Columbia, New York, and Quebec, and some driving rental cars have flown in from all over the world.

What we glimpse in these dining images is not a melancholy event nostalgically recalled, but a glimpse of what the eschatological reign of God will look like. It is just a hint of what cannot, of course, be described directly, but only indirectly. But even using such down-to-earth images, we can catch a glimpse of what a new creation might look like—a healed and repaired creation, represented by the messianic banquet.

The sacrament is layered enough that its tone will not be exactly the same on Maundy Thursday as it is on Easter Sunday. And of course it can be more than one thing at the same time, but it will always point ahead of itself to that ultimate "feast of victory for our God," when *"we shall feast with all your saints in the joy of your eternal realm."*

The Great Thanksgiving ends with a Trinitarian ascription of praise, such as this one:

> All praise and glory are yours,
> > Holy One of Israel,
> > Word of God incarnate,
> > Power of the Most High,
> > one God, now and forever.[5]

And the people join in, adding their *Amen!*

---

5. Evangelical Lutheran Church in America, *Evangelical Lutheran Worship*, Setting One: 3, 110.

8

Preaching When Naiveté Has Fled

Sacramentality

THE WORD OF GOD read and PREACHED is sacramental just as the holy meal is. "Sacramental" means that each of the two primary movements of the liturgy is meant to serve the shared purpose of discovering a kind of meeting place between God and the assembled church. In the service of the word of God, God reaches out to us by means of biblical text and human speech, which we pray that the Spirit will use to establish a connection that runs deeper and truer than is possible when superficially processing language. In the Eucharist, we pray that God will draw near in the nourishing ways that feed us heart and soul in what we might rightly be described as "body language." Luther believed that

> God's word always attaches itself to something created, even to something physical. As a form of self-communication from person to person, it is never disembodied. The word may be in the text of the Bible, the mouth of the preacher, or the earthly elements of the sacraments. The Word that was incarnated in Jesus the Christ, the divine Logos, is always taking on flesh not only in the way it is conveyed, but also in the life of the believer who receives it . . . But such communication is never only verbal. It is just as "real," just as "living," when it is conveyed through those sacramental signs that are also forms of the word of God, the divine self-communication.[1]

---

1. Senn, *Christian Liturgy*, 306–7.

John Calvin's view is similar.

> Therefore, let it be regarded as a settled principle that the sacraments have the same office as the Word of God; to offer and set forth Christ to us, and in him the treasures of heavenly grace.[2]

The following story is an example of what "sacramental" looks like.

A Preacher's Reflections of a Liturgical Sort: "Won't Jesus Miss Us?"

The father of a parishioner told me a family story. His two daughters had left the nest. His adult son, who was intellectually challenged, remained at home. Every Sunday, the couple and their son worshiped with a Lutheran congregation. One week, for some reason, circumstances required that they stay home, and the father told his son that they would not be going to church that day. The young man was uncharacteristically silent for a time, and then worriedly asked, "Won't Jesus miss us?"

It was a touching question, one that highlighted the simplicity of the young man and the charm of what seemed to be his naiveté. With reflection on the story over time, it has come to seem to me that it reveals something profoundly important. The young man's unguarded description of how he experienced the church at worship is a reminder of what has dimmed for many of us in a secular age, or even been lost.

We live in a society in which "truth" is hotly contested. It is this politics against another politics, this tribe against another, my certainty against yours, one claim of authority against other claims, and plenty of suspicion of each other to go around. When society has fallen out of love with the faith with which it had been more or less acquainted for generations, it can seem that even the presider's greeting, "The Lord be with you," is subject to debate.

It is unfortunately too common that we go to worship as though we were going to a classroom that has been made a bit more welcoming with a bit of music. We may be looking forward to learning the lesson we expect to hear from the pulpit, or we may simply bear it, but what we expect, in any occasion, is to be taught something. No wonder that a nine-year-old, told that the family must go to church on Sunday since it will be Easter, responded that he didn't need to go, since he already knew what Easter

---

2. Calvin, *Inst.* 4:14.17.

means. The lesson having been mastered, no repetition of it was necessary. At an early age, the boy has already acquired the sense that worship is basically a kind of school.

While it is true that when we are paying attention we are quite likely to learn something in worship, the acquiring of information is basically a side benefit, not the main point. Ironically, it is the intellectually challenged young man who got the point. He is not equipped with the mental tools for processing information that is the least complicated. In church, he does not bring any expectation of learning much that is new to him, or finding intellectual support for the faith he already has. Since both of these capacities are important for most of the rest of us, his deficits may arouse our pity. However, it might be worth saving some of that pity for ourselves, who have our own deficits. Because, having been so carefully taught to doubt any conviction that cannot be demonstrated in a manner that passes for "proof," we have unplugged a part of the original equipment with which we were born.

One might dare to go so far as to say that relentless cultural programming has caused us to disable parts of ourselves. Those inborn capacities that enable us to meld intuition and experience (without disarming our reasoning powers) have been nearly shut down, especially when it comes to our dealings with God. These capacities are still accessible when it comes to everyday relationships, so they are not entirely missing. But when it comes to the really big picture, the ultimate relationship, we are likely to find ourselves at a loss. The young man who worries that Jesus might "miss us" is *enabled* precisely where many of us are disabled.

When he goes to church, he is immersed in a bath of experiences that he welcomes and embraces without worrying about testing them intellectually. It is not in his nature to be suspicious of what he senses and feels. Of course, this means that he is vulnerable, and his vulnerability requires protection from those who care about him. But vulnerability is appropriate in certain circumstances. Letting down one's defensiveness, one's guardedness, whether intellectual or emotional, is an essential component in the formation of our deepest relationships, certainly including the one with the holy God. "Truly I tell you, whoever does not receive the kingdom of God as a little child will never enter it" (Mark 10:15).

For the young man to worry that the Jesus he knows most intimately from church might "miss us," is to draw attention to his sense of the presence of the risen Christ. Jesus Christ is present to us, and we are present to him in and through our being present to one another. The young man is welcomed at church, and, finding a place in the assembly, he is included as an equal rather than separated from those whose abilities are different from his. He knows the sung and spoken responses, cued by familiar words, all engraved on his heart, never to be forgotten to the end of his life. He knows when to say the Amen. He joins in song as best he can, unrehearsed, with those who can carry a tune and those who can't. He receives and offers the Peace, hand in hand, face to face.

If he is so fortunate as to be in a worshiping congregation that understands that worship is offered in and with the body as well as in the head, he will have mastered the commonplace gestures and movements that represent a body language that can speak as profoundly as spoken words. He can make the sign of the cross, open his hands and spread them during prayer, bow when the triune God is evoked. He will join the parade moving toward the bread and cup, bodily rehearsing the lifelong, shared journey toward the heavenly feast. And, as he moves with the others, he will see the body of Christ, young and old, faithful and not-so-much, in whatever diversity is represented in that place. He will receive the gifts of bread and cup; will taste and see that the Lord is good. He will be expecting the Blessing offered at the dismissal, and never worry that he might have fallen short on sincerity here and there, or been distracted, or otherwise offended God by a momentary lapse of attention. In short, he will be present, and embrace presence, naturally and without self-consciousness.

In an era marked by an uneasy skepticism about churches and about faith itself, those who are not yet ready to give it up find themselves looking for reasoned support for not throwing in the towel. But it has always been and still remains true that faith is not something we have been reasoned into. Yes, of course, we can find arguments to support our faith, but normally faith comes first, followed by a lifetime of mentally organizing the reasons that strengthen it. Faith is reasonable, so to speak, but it is more than an opinion about God, Christ, and holy things. As such, faith is a response to a whole complex of experiences, some involving reasoning, others coming to us in subtle ways for which there may be no unambiguous explanation. To speak about it at all requires a variety of imaginative uses of language that exhibit the same kind of truthful subtlety as a painting does, or a hymn, or a carefully crafted story.

Worship has never been intended to be either a classroom or a concert hall. The Bible is not a textbook. Liturgical language is not the language of engineering or journalism. Worship is meant to be a meeting place. It is a place of "presence." I am not talking about emotion, necessarily, nor excluding it either. Not talking about a method of inducing a spiritual high, or otherwise surrendering one's intellect.

Those who know at least a little about church talk know that "presence" is likely to be the sort of language expected when we talk about the sacraments. But preaching is also about presence. Preaching is not just lecturing on a religious or ethical subject, not exhorting, not motivational speaking, not explaining the historical context of Second Kings or Second Corinthians. Those things will happen, but they play only a supporting role in a unique kind of speech. The intention of this speech is to lead us to a state of attentiveness to the God who offers us a place of meeting in and through language carefully used.

The starting place for preaching is the language of the Bible. Biblical language has human fingerprints all over it. One can see it as a piece of art, not unlike other arts such as music, dance, or poetry, projecting meaning in ways that are sometimes subtle, speaking to us at levels of our being sometimes different from the ways we communicate with reasoned words, but not in conflict with them. Biblical language draws attention to the God who is able to be present to us in, through, and in spite of the limitations inherent in human speech. Sometimes, it uses indirection as the most direct means to create a meeting place. It invites us to be present to God, Christ, Spirit.

Preaching becomes its best self when in the original and normal context of the sacramental meal, which serves as an invitation and foretaste of the meal to be shared, ultimately, by predator and prey alike, reconciled in the peaceable kingdom. Preaching is what the meal would be were it to be consumed in words only, and the sacramental meal points to and embraces that One whose life, death, resurrection, and coming reign is meant to be central in our preaching.

Lord George MacLeod, a minister of the Church of Scotland, founded the Iona Community in 1938. He was pastor of a church in Glasgow that served a neighborhood in which most people worked with their hands. No doubt they were bright people, but in worship, the need to process spoken language proved ineffective when wordiness so dominated the service that it drowned out the language of the heart. MacLeod struggled to understand how to minister to them in worship, and concluded that a way to do that might be to recover a lost treasure—a celebration of the sacramental meal every Sunday, sermon and sacrament, side-by-side, a layering of languages that, while including words, was also soul language, body language, heart language. Each language illuminated and enhanced the others. The glory of the Word was made manifest in ordinary speech and also in the same Word made manifest in action: taking, breaking, giving thanks, and nourishing the hungry faithful in bread and wine: Jesus Christ, our food and drink.

"Won't Jesus miss us?" The young man serves to remind us of what we have so often lost: an inborn capacity to see and welcome God among us in the language of "doing" as well as in the language of the thoughtful mind (Luke 22:19). Paul Ricoeur has reminded us that, when we have lost confidence in the naiveté of our childhood, there is nevertheless the possibility for what he calls a "second naiveté." That sounds to me like setting aside our culturally induced suspicion of the peculiarities of the necessary languages of worship, both those spoken and unspoken. Particularly, permitting ourselves to enter less guardedly into worship in its "being" mode. Whether it is the language of bread and wine or the language of Bible, prayer, and preaching, it is all offered as one great meal, refreshment in our inevitable wildernesses.[3]

A Preacher's Reflections: Second Naiveté

At some time or other, our daughters and sons have to come to terms with Santa Claus and to a lesser extent, with the Easter Bunny. Most of us start out as earnest believers. As time passes, we collect more information. We go to our parents with questions. Our questions make them uncomfortable, and they fumble around for something that will satisfy us. Sooner or later, we find that we have to revise our early naiveté. Revise it, or sacrifice it.

It seems as though growing up is a constant process of disillusionment. We began by imagining our parents as all-powerful, even god-like. Children are impressed by authorities—teachers, team captains, quarterbacks, cheerleaders, doctors, pastors, presidents. When I was a child, the world was filled with mysteries—mostly beyond my understanding, but all either wonderful or scary. A little bit at a time, as we mature, what people call "realism" sets in. When my siblings and I reached adulthood, we used to sit around and analyze our parents—slowly, reluctantly learning to see them as very human beings. But it turns out that when you yourself become

---

3. This is a lightly edited version of a story that first appeared in *The Presbyterian Outlook* in 2020.

a figure of authority, or get close to being perceived as one, every authority figure diminishes in size. The "mysteries" are explainable, the wonder has evaporated, nothing is what we first thought it to be.

Growing up is, for some at least, a series of disenchantments. This is true also in matters of faith. As childhood gives way to adolescence, and adolescence to young adulthood, we've got to figure out what to do with that early faith. As we collect more information, as we gather more experience in the world, we have to make some revisions—or throw it out altogether. Those who are reluctant to throw it out altogether may revise too hastily. Maybe it is possible to figure out a way to square our early faith with what passes for "common sense." So, the biblical God, who parts seas and gathers a people and comes into the world *incognito* in Bethlehem, and heals the sick and turns a crucifixion upside down—this God is reduced to an abstraction, a "higher power," a holy blur, a faceless, nameless, Hallmark sentimentality. This distant God is not unlike the "spirit of giving" that parents struggle to substitute for Saint Nick. Somehow, the substitutions don't work very well. They leave us with the taste of disappointment.

I have been troubled for years with the ways some try to salvage the wreckage of their faith by planing it down as they might plane in the wood shop, smoothing the rough edges, then hammering until the square peg of their faith fits the round hole of conventional wisdom. So we end up with a low-fat faith, a reduced faith, one that stands for nothing more than what everybody already knew anyway. The final result is something so bland, so undemanding, so superficial that one wonders whether it is worth salvaging in the first place.

In high school a Catholic friend told me the story of Our Lady of Fatima. Supposedly, the Virgin Mary had appeared to a Spanish schoolgirl in 1917, entrusting her with a secret message. The message was to be revealed in a specific year—maybe it was 1965. If I remember correctly, the message turned out to be something like, "pray the Rosary each day to bring peace to the world." Now, no one could doubt that prayer for peace in the world is desirable, but such an admonition is not rare. In fact, that prayerful longing is no doubt as old as conflict itself. Something that might have been expected to be quite marvelous turned out to be banal—not unworthy, yet ordinary enough to be disappointing.

Even in the first century, there were folks around who wanted to take the rough edges off the Christian gospel. They were called gnostics, and they were offended by the idea of a crucified Lord. They preferred a bloodless faith, one without sweat or passion, one that could be reduced to an antiseptic wisdom—even better, a secret wisdom handed down from heaven to a few folks who were "in the know." In the days of the early church, St. John found himself standing up against those who tried to clean the gospel up, make it daintier, more socially acceptable. John's struggle with Gnosticism comes into focus when his Gospel reports Jesus to have said, "Very truly I tell you, unless you eat the flesh of the Son of Man and drink his blood, you have no life in you" (John 6:53).

This statement, on the face of it, is offensive. It goes against our need for a polite, inoffensive delicacy of speech. Isn't it gruesome to speak of eating Christ's flesh and drinking his blood? It is disturbing, off-putting to those whose imaginations are inclined to be literal. But it is precisely in its offensiveness that we either perceive the truth of it or miss it altogether. The Christian gospel, it turns out, is not just a certain kind of commonplace advice about how to be nice. It isn't just platitudes warmed over. It is not just one more exhortation to behave ourselves. The Christian gospel is not something that everybody knows already; is not something we could easily figure out on our own; is not "reasonable" by the standards of any society.

When her college history teacher commented that Christianity was not reasonable, the student was shocked. Troubled and questioning, the student appealed to a member of the Religion Department. That professor chose not to dispute the observation of the history professor. He explained that certainly one might argue that Christianity is not "reasonable." But it is not foolish, either, or without reason. What is given in the gospel comes to us from God. We did not reason it out from scratch by ourselves. It exceeds the investigatory power available to us from human reason alone. "For God's foolishness is wiser than human wisdom, and God's weakness is stronger than human strength" (1 Cor 1:25).

In John's Gospel, Jesus speaks in a jarring manner that supports the contention that the gospel cannot be reduced to an exercise of the intellect alone. It is not just about a way of thinking. The gospel is about where to find nourishment. Where we find nourishment, according to the Christian gospel, is in the person of Jesus Christ himself. It is Jesus himself whom God sets before us to meet a hunger that is experienced even before we know how to identify it. What God offers in the gospel is not a new set of ideas, or even a new moral agenda or a whole new list of obligations. What God offers us is God's own self in this person, Jesus Christ. What God offers is this One who both attracts and offends; this One who arouses deep loyalties and fierce antagonisms; this One who stirs up the rage of those whose job it is to defend the *status quo*. What God offers is not abstract philosophizing, but this particular person, whom the authorities subjected to the death penalty—this specific person, who could not be put down, but who made the journey from life to death and to life again, and promised us that we, too, shall make that journey. In short, the gospel is nothing more nor less than God's hand stretched out to us in this particular person, Jesus of Nazareth, God's Christ. He is the food and drink God has provided for us, in this wilderness and all the others.

Lord, to Whom Shall We Go?

We like to talk about what we had for dinner, and to compare menus and restaurants. Food is important in every society. It is not just about calories—it is about aesthetics, it is about friendship, it is about closeness. Where we go for nourishment tells a lot about us. Fast food, gourmet, home-cooked—each has its own appeal.

It is in that light that we need to understand Jesus' choice of this particular extended figure of speech, whether the words are his own or chosen by John to represent what the church had received in their experience of Jesus. "Those who eat my flesh and drink my blood have eternal life" (John 6:54). In other words, our nourishing relationship with Jesus Christ is just as crucial to our spiritual vitality as the food we eat is to our physical vitality. It means that our relation to this Jesus Christ is absolutely critical for us. It is not just a relationship of the intellect. Not a neutral, objective relationship, not one that is without risks or one that makes us invulnerable. It is a relationship so vital, so close to the soul, so sustaining that it is more accurate to speak of it as something we consume, to be absorbed in our inner being.

Jesus' vivid language precipitated a crisis. "Because of this," John tells us, "many of his disciples turned back and no longer went about with him" (John 6:66). But the twelve—those who knew him best—said, "Lord, to whom can we go? You have the words of eternal life" (6:68). And this is exactly the point, isn't it? What God offers us in Jesus Christ does not fit easily into our preconceived notions of what we need or where we think we might get it. It may seem that what we need is something like a title on the door, or the newest technology, a strong portfolio, and someplace to retreat on the weekends. We think we are owed explanations—why things are as they are, and how they will become what they will become. We think we need something to immunize us against the pitfalls of life. But what God thinks we need is something else: heavenly food, sustenance for the soul. And God has given that in Jesus of Nazareth.

Puzzled, but not Bereft

The young man, intellectually disabled, who was fearful that Jesus would "miss" him and his family, has absorbed this truth. Perhaps it is more accurate to say that he intuits it, because it is not in his power to explain it. He intuits it, "gets it" because he is receptive in some ways that ought to matter to all of us. For us who find ourselves immersed in a culture for which explanations and proofs are essential when speaking of important things, we are easily confused when addressed by One who speaks to us over, under, and around the conventional uses of human speech. Puzzled we may be, but we are not entirely bereft, because there is help wrapped in the illuminating gift of the "second naiveté." That is, we can allow ourselves to discover how to trust the signals of our hearts just enough to become newly enabled as we turn toward the promised banquet.

"Those who eat my flesh and drink my blood have eternal life, and I will raise them up on the last day" (6:54). We will not see the truth of this absolutely and for sure and beyond dispute until "the last day." This affirmation was in dispute back then and it is in dispute now, and yet people of faith learn to trust it because there is soul food here, and we have already sampled it. "Lord, to whom can we go?" "If naiveté means absence of guile . . . it is a quality for which Christians ought to strive. One way to do so is to approach Scripture "naively," trusting its imagery and hyperbole to form one's own imagination."[4]

"O taste and see that the LORD is good" (Ps 34:8a).

Trying on a "Second Naiveté"

Children, dressing up or pretending to dress up, like to try on roles. They imitate authority figures—a parent, teacher, athlete, doctor, nurse, truck driver, the engineer on the train that passes through town.

---

4. Green, *Imagining Theology*, 203.

> Worship can be a kind of trying on of roles. In reality, our individual faith waxes and wanes, vacillates between confidence and uncertainty. The liturgy invites us to try on the role of a faithful person. We can try on that role in several ways, by singing, speaking, moving, gesturing. We can try on the role of belonging to the great community of the faithful, gathered before the throne of God, with angels and archangels, and the whole company of heaven. We can try on the role of those who have been invited from east and west and from north and south to sit at the great Messianic banquet. We can try on the role of those who gather by the river that flows from the throne of God. The liturgy invites us to that playfulness that gives permission to imagine ourselves as God's royal priesthood, God's chosen people, a communion of saints for whom the boundary between time and eternity is permeable. It invites us to imagine ourselves as part of a healed creation, a new heaven and earth, in which nothing lies outside God's redemptive power, not even hell itself, where Christ has gone to preach to the prisoners.[5]

Preaching, embedded in the liturgy of the church, offers an invitation to those assembled to join in the adventure of trying on a more trusting, less-guarded, intellectually grown up—indeed, a critical naiveté— to see how it fits.

---

5. Byars, *Future of Protestant Worship*, 34.

Afterword

When Mere Words Become Bread and Wine

In the presence of God and of Christ Jesus, who is to judge the living and the dead, and in view of his appearing and his kingdom, I solemnly urge you: proclaim the message; be persistent whether the time is favorable or unfavorable. (2 Tim 4:1–2)

A Preacher's Reflection: Favorable, or Unfavorable?

How would you describe the time in which we live? Favorable? Or unfavorable? There's a sense in which these times are decidedly unfavorable. There is a kind of secularism at work in our society that might be described as fundamentalist. One can have a fundamentalist mindset without being religious. A fundamentalist kind of secularism is a species of blind certainty that there is no God—or at least, no God of the sort known by Christians or Jews. No God that anybody will have to account to; no God of whom we expect anything at all.

And side by side with this strident secularism, there can be too much religiosity. Say, a gullibility that latches on to anything that describes itself as "spiritual," without much discrimination, and certainly without any expectation of long-term fidelity to one's vision at the moment. "Spirituality" is "in," while the biblical God is "out." The exception being the religious right, who appeal to chapter and verse to smite their enemies, among whom are most of the historic Christian churches. From no faith at all, to an undiscriminating credulousness, to neurotic religion—that's one description of our time. Is it a "favorable" time? Or "unfavorable"?

Afterword

Whatever you decide about that, the fact is that our era is a whole lot like the period we read about in the New Testament. The early Christians had to deal with the same sorts of forces: no faith, undiscriminating spiritual conventionality, and the kind of faith that is scary when it goes neurotic. It was in just that sort of environment that Christian faith began its first healthy growth. Maybe that suggests that every time is both favorable and unfavorable for the hearing of the gospel. Our time may seem to be one of bare, ruined altars. And yet, it is also a time when people are starving—hungry—for what? Some word from the Lord? So, is this time one that is unfavorable? Or favorable?

Maybe Both

It is no longer news that church membership has declined, or that Christian faith is no longer respected in the measure that it had been for generations. The likelihood is that the church of the future will be smaller. And yet, this is not altogether bad news. It has always been the case, certainly at least since the time of Constantine, that adherents to the church vary a good deal in their levels of commitment to the faith. When Constantine lifted up the persecuted church in the fourth century to make it the favored religion of the empire, it was as though there were a new Starbucks in town—all sorts of people got in line to join up. Speculation estimates that about a third of them were devout; another third believed, but less intensely; and another third were just going along with the program. I suspect that the proportions have always been something like that, and where the numbers drop off, they start dropping off a long way before you get to the first group and maybe even the second. It is likely that, as our culture no longer has any overt spiritual expectations of its members, the outer circle will fall away from the church sooner or later. Nevertheless, while the crowds will be thinner, the core is likely to hold.

Jesus' words are just as trustworthy now as they were in the days before they dragged him out to silence him for good. Just as reliable as they proved to be on the day when he broke the chains of death. We don't need to worry about it. Jesus' promise will be just as reliable in a secular era as in apparently pious times. Certainly there will always be many who simply won't get it, and don't need any longer to pretend to get it—most of them quite honorable persons. But the word is still reliable: The Lord Jesus who calls his own by name will not call out in vain. There shall never fail to be a response. "My sheep hear my voice. I know them, and they follow me. . . . No one will snatch them out of my hand" (John 10:27–28b).

Nevertheless, that likely means smaller memberships, fewer congregations, and budgets no longer supplemented by those in the outer ring. However, those who remain are likely to be those who are willing to be, in a sense, non-conforming as far as the cultural *Zeitgeist* goes. They will be more willing to study and learn, more willing to worship regularly and more available to share in the church's corporate calling to serve the world. And, always there have been some people who may be indifferent to cultural expectations and more willing to pay serious attention to those who have something to say that does not fall within the boundaries of the usual conventionalities. Some of these may find themselves drawn to churches that show themselves to be theologically serious, for whom God really matters. The likelihood, then, is that there will be numerical losses, but other opportunities for gains.

In these uncertain times for the church, what are we going to do? After Jesus' ascension, the disciples hardly knew what to do. Scripture tells us that they returned to Jerusalem. "When they had entered the city, they went to the room upstairs where they were staying. . . . All these were constantly devoting themselves to prayer, together with certain women . . . as well as his brothers" (Acts 1:13–14).

It was a critical moment, that pause after the ascension. But might they have proved themselves wise to have delayed awhile, rather than to have gone running off in the wrong direction? Even when it may have seemed that some urgency was required? And so, the disciples and the friends and family of Jesus waited before God; waited for something new to be given. They waited for God to clear their minds of traditional expectations and show them at least a beginning-point for an entirely new agenda.

I think that the church as we know it may also have reached such a point: a point where, in our race to rescue the faith, it may be better to pause; a point in which it is appropriate to wait before God and the possibility that familiar patterns of relating to the world, of being Christian in the world, may be reshaped. The future of the "mainline" will emerge as it lays aside nostalgic memories of its former semi-establishment status, and embraces a new identity as a non-establishment kind of church.

The disciples, in their upper room, feeling empty after Jesus' ascension, waited prayerfully before God for something new to be given. And, of course, we who know the Pentecost story know that before long something new *was* given. The church in our time, too, if we pause before God, and pray for some clarity, shall certainly know the sweetness of something new: some new way of being in the world and for the world, a people of faith and a people of integrity amid the cross-currents of loud and over-confident voices. In going forward, we circle back to seek encouragement once again in the miracle of Pentecost, and the power of the Holy Spirit.

A Preacher's Reflections: The Spirit of Hope

Today we are immersed in a vast ocean of words. We hear them, but don't hear them. Seeing a commercial for the hundredth time, we are stumped if someone should ask what product it is meant to sell. The ever-lengthening election seasons are a nightmare of words strung together in overdrive. The fact is, in twenty-first-century America, words are cheap. They advocate, they protest, they deceive, they inform, they obscure, they manipulate, they cheat, they soothe, they reassure, they scold, they promise, they disgust, and they delight. There are so many words, and they are so easily bent to a dubious purpose. Only a few of them actually cross the threshold of our conscious attention.

There was a time, in what seems the distant past, when words were not cheap. In oral societies, lengthy genealogies, ancestral stories, songs, and proverbs were memorized in precise detail. Not a precious word was lost in the oral transmission from one generation to another. It should not be surprising that preaching played a powerful role in societies that were predominantly oral cultures. Respect for the spoken language remained widespread even well into the twentieth century.

The newly minted pastor soon discovers the limitations of the preacher's calling. Congregations have learned to be suspicious of words. Because words are as often used against us as they are used for us, and because words are so frequently crafted to deceive and to manipulate, those who are in the pews bring less trust to our listening than perhaps they did in another time.

St. Francis is remembered as having said, "Preach the gospel at all times. Use words if necessary." The fact is that a time *does* come when words are necessary. The church can minister to the sick and comfort the dying. The church can feed the hungry and clothe the naked—and it must. But should someone ask why we are doing this, it turns out that we do need words. Words to testify to the God who calms the storms and raises the dead. Words to speak of the God who joins us in the cross-shaped places and lifts us into the resurrection life. Words to speak of promises made. Words that summon, call, conscript, commission, and equip.

One of the crises of the church as we experience it today is a crisis of words, of language, of speech. In a time when words are cheap, when they are suspect, we may find ourselves disarmed, unequipped, not able to trust ourselves to use our very own language. If we speak of God, we expect to be met with scorn or indifference. If we speak of death and resurrection, we expect to be met with skepticism. We don't expect to be convincing, don't expect anyone to believe us, and feel sure that we will make no converts, win no hearts and no minds. Let the Evangelism Committee do it; let the Committee on Church Growth do it. Surely there are experts among us who will know what to say! The rest of us are hard-pressed even to venture a "Hello, and welcome!" to a visitor at church for fear of coming on too strong.

It is hard to imagine the little company of disciples in Jerusalem on the first Pentecost after Jesus' death, resurrection, and ascension. They had been in hiding, fearful of the authorities, scared that there were other crosses to be brought out of storage to bear the weight of the next body. The apostles had something to say, of course. But how would they say it?

Words are hard to find when we need them to bear the weight of holy things. There is nothing rational, nothing understandable about resurrection of the dead. Nothing comprehensible about a God who descended into a cross-shaped place, a God who turns death inside out, who called this one person, Jesus of Nazareth, out of death's dark prison specifically as a promise of a transfigured creation. No human language is up to the task.

The Pentecost story tells about the empowerment of the powerless disciples, whose only advantage might be the power of their testimony. Luke, the writer of Acts, means us to understand that what happened that day is not about some special skill possessed by the apostles. They had not been secretly studying at Duolingo, or working with phrase books or Google Translate to learn how to say "risen from the dead" in Coptic or Latin or Arabic. It was quite otherwise. Luke tells the story of a violent *pneuma*, a fierce wind or spirit that, if one could have seen it, might have looked like tongues of fire. Fire that burned, but did not consume, like the burning bush at which Moses was confronted by the One who self-identified as "I AM."

Afterword

> All of them were filled with the Holy Spirit and began to speak in other languages, as the Spirit gave them ability. (Acts 2:4)

The Holy Spirit can do things like that. Our speech is a clumsy tool, not up to the task, *unless our speech should be transformed by the Holy Spirit*.

In worship, we are taught to pray for the help of the Holy Spirit before reading from Scripture and preaching, because apart from the Spirit, words are just sounds. It does not matter that they come from the Bible; or that they may come from the preacher's heart. Words are nothing more than sounds battering the ear until the Spirit enables them to find a lodging in mind and soul. The Holy Spirit takes the ordinary stuff of human speech, and turns it into the equivalent of bread and wine. Bread to strengthen the one who feeds on it; wine to gladden the heart.

Certainly, Luke did not write the story of that first Christian Pentecost the same way a newspaper reporter might have written it. Probably there is in Luke's draft both a little history and a little parable. The disciples took a risk. They went public. They spoke in words that could hardly be expected to hit home in the multilingual crowds celebrating the festival. But they must have been words about God's providential hand; about how God had transformed the shame of the cross; words about the risen Christ as both the fulfillment of an existing promise and of a new one: that of a transfigured creation. They must have spoken about the risen Christ having trampled death underfoot. They must have uttered out loud the dangerous and subversive testimony: "Jesus is Lord." How could anyone, at that time, or this, be reasonably expected to understand (much less welcome) all those curious words? But, the Spirit used the apostles' speech, and it became bread and wine for the soul. Those who needed to hear, heard.

It is not time for us to give up on the Holy Spirit. It is not time to give up on the story that is bread and wine for us. It is true that the churches find themselves in a very different place than in decades or centuries past. However, as clumsy as our speech may be, theologically sophisticated or not, perfectly adjusted to the times or not, our words may, under the right circumstances, become bread and wine for one or many who desperately need the nourishment and joy of the gospel. When we offer whatever words are available to us, whatever speech comes naturally, the Spirit may cause the words to bear fruit beyond our power either to imagine or control. People whom we may expect to be skeptical if not actually scornful may yet be able to say with us, "in our own languages we hear them speaking about God's deeds of power" (Acts 2:11).

> I looked, and there was a great multitude that no one could count, from every nation, from all tribes and peoples and languages, standing before the throne and before the Lamb, robed in white, with palm branches in their hands. They cried out in a loud voice, saying, "Salvation belongs to our God who is seated on the throne, and to the Lamb!" (Rev 7:9–10)

Bibliography

Antiochian Orthodox Christian Archdiocese of North America. *The Liturgikon: The Book of Divine Services for the Priest and Deacon*. 2nd ed. New York: Athens, 1989.
Bainton, Roland H. *Here I Stand: A Life of Martin Luther*. New York: Abingdon, 1950.
Barth, Karl. *The Preaching of the Gospel*. Translated by B. E. Hooke. Philadelphia: Westminster, 1963.
Bauckham, Richard. *Jesus and the Eyewitnesses: The Gospels as Eyewitness Testimony*. 2nd ed. Grand Rapids: Eerdmans, 2017.
Bolz-Weber, Nadia. *Pastrix: The Cranky, Beautiful Faith of a Sinner & Saint*. New York: Hatchette, 2013.
Brooks, David. "You Are Not Who You Think You Are." *New York Times*, September 3, 2021. https://www.nytimes.com/2021/09/02/opinion/brain-reality-imagination.html.
Byars, Ronald P. *Believer on Sunday, Atheist by Thursday: Is Faith Still Possible?* Eugene, OR: Cascade, 2019.
———. *Finding Our Balance: Repositioning Mainstream Protestantism*. Eugene, OR: Cascade, 2015.
———. *The Future of Protestant Worship: Beyond the Worship Wars*. Louisville: Westminster John Knox, 2002.
———. *The Sacraments in Biblical Perspective*. Louisville: Westminster John Knox, 2011.
Calvin, John. *Institutes of the Christian Religion*. Edited by John T. McNeill. Translated by Ford Lewis Battles. Philadelphia: Westminster, 1960.
Carroll, John T. *Luke: A Commentary*. New Testament Library. Louisville: Westminster John Knox, 2012.
Church of Scotland. *Book of Common Order of the Church of Scotland*. Edinburgh: Saint Andrew, 1994.
Davis, Ellen F. *Wondrous Depth: Preaching the Old Testament*. Louisville: Westminster John Knox, 2005.
Du Mez, Kristin Kobes. *Jesus and John Wayne: How White Evangelicals Corrupted a Faith and Fractured a Nation*. New York: Liveright, 2020.
Episcopal Church. *The Book of Common Prayer and Administration of the Sacraments and Other Rites and Ceremonies of the Church according to the Use of the Episcopal Church*. New York: The Church Hymnal Corporation, 1979.
Evangelical Lutheran Church in America. *Evangelical Lutheran Worship*. Minneapolis: Augsburg Fortress, 2006.

Bibliography

Frei, Hans W. *Theology and Narrative: Selected Essays*. Edited by George Hunsinger and William C. Placher. New York: Oxford University Press, 1993.

Green, Garrett. *Imagining Theology: Encounters with God in Scripture, Interpretation, and Aesthetics*. Grand Rapids: Baker Academic, 2020.

Hageman, Howard G. *Pulpit and Table*. Richmond, VA: John Knox, 1962.

Hart, David Bentley. *Atheist Delusions: The Christian Revolution and Its Fashionable Enemies*. New Haven: Yale University Press, 2009.

———. *That All Shall Be Saved: Heaven, Hell, and Universal Salvation*. New Haven: Yale University Press, 2019.

Hurtado, Larry W. *Destroyer of the Gods: Early Christian Distinctiveness in the Roman World*. Waco: Baylor University Press, 2016.

Jasper, R. D. D., and G. J. Cuming. *Prayers of the Eucharist: Early and Reformed*. 3rd ed. Collegeville, MN: Liturgical, 1990.

Johnson, Luke Timothy. *Miracles: God's Presence and Power in Creation*. Louisville: Westminster John Knox, 2018.

Jones, Serene. *Calvin and the Rhetoric of Piety*. Louisville: Westminster John Knox, 1995.

Jungmann, Joseph A. *The Mass of the Roman Rite: Its Origins and Development*. New York: Benziger, 1959.

Lutheran Church in America. *Lutheran Book of Worship*. Minister's Desk Edition. Minneapolis: Board of Publication, Lutheran Church in America, 2000.

Mazza, Enrico. *The Eucharistic Prayers of the Roman Rite*. Translated by Matthew J. O'Connell. New York: Pueblo, 1986.

Newbigin, Lesslie. *The Gospel in a Pluralist Society*. Grand Rapids: Eerdmans, 1989.

———. *Proper Confidence: Faith, Doubt and Certainty in Christian Discipleship*. Grand Rapids: Eerdmans, 1995.

Presbyterian Church in Canada. *Book of Common Worship: The Presbyterian Church in Canada*. N.p.: Presbyterian Church in Canada, 1991.

Presbyterian Church (USA). "The Confession of 1967." In *The Constitution of the Presbyterian Church (U.S.A.). Part 1: Book of Confessions*, 80–85. Louisville: Office of the General Assembly, 2002.

———. "Great Thanksgiving: 2." In *Book of Common Worship*, 122–23. Louisville: Westminster John Knox, 2018.

———. "Great Thanksgiving J." In *Book of Common Worship*, 156. Louisville: Westminster John Knox, 1993.

———. *Service for the Lord's Day and Lectionary for the Christian Year*. Philadelphia: Westminster, 1964.

Ramshaw, Gail. "The Long and Short of Eucharistic Praying." *Call to Worship: Liturgy, Music, Preaching & the Arts* 40.4 (2007) 32–36.

Rutledge, Fleming. *And God Spoke to Abraham: Preaching from the Old Testament*. Grand Rapids: Eerdmans, 2011.

———. *The Crucifixion: Understanding the Death of Jesus Christ*. Grand Rapids: Eerdmans, 2015.

Schmemann, Alexander. *The Eucharist: Sacrament of the Kingdom*. Translated by Paul Kachur. Crestwood, NY: St. Vladimir's Seminary Press, 1987.

Senn, Frank C. *Christian Liturgy: Catholic and Evangelical*. Minneapolis: Fortress, 1997.

Smith, James K. A. *How (Not) to Be Secular: Reading Charles Taylor*. Grand Rapids: Eerdmans, 2014.

Bibliography

Stark, Rodney. *The Rise of Christianity: How the Obscure, Marginal Jesus Movement Became the Dominant Religious Force in the Western World in a Few Centuries.* San Francisco: HarperSanFrancisco, 1997.
Taylor, Charles. *A Secular Age.* Cambridge, MA: Belknap, 2007.
Thompson, Bard. *Liturgies of the Western Church.* Philadelphia: Fortress, 1961.
Torrance, Thomas F. *Space, Time and Resurrection.* Edinburgh: T. & T. Clark, 1976.
Tyler, Anne. *A Patchwork Planet.* New York: Knopf, 1998.
United Church of Christ. *Book of Worship: United Church of Christ.* New York: United Church of Christ Office for Church Life and Leadership, 1986.
———. *The Lord's Day Service with Explanatory Notes.* Philadelphia: United Church Press, 1964.
United Methodist Book of Worship. Nashville: United Methodist Publishing House, 1992.
United Methodist Church. "The Great Thanksgiving for Advent." In *United Methodist Book of Worship*, 54–55. Nashville: United Methodist Publishing House, 1992.
Volf, Miroslav. "Proclaiming the Lord's Death." *Christian Century* 116.7 (1999) 253.
Wehner, Peter. "Will Christian America Withstand the Pull of QAnon?" *The New York Times*, June 18, 2021. https://www.nytimes.com/2021/06/18/opinion/southern-baptist-convention-christianity.html.
Willimon, William H. *How Odd of God: Chosen for the Curious Vocation of Preaching.* Louisville: Westminster John Knox, 2015.
Wright, N. T. *The Day the Revolution Began: Reconsidering the Meaning of Jesus's Crucifixion.* San Francisco: HarperOne, 2016.

www.ingramcontent.com/pod-product-compliance
Lightning Source LLC
Chambersburg PA
CBHW031500160426
43195CB00010BB/1040